Latin Alive

Fr. Francisco Radecki, CMRI

ISBN-10: 0988274418

ISBN-13: 978-0-9882744-1-9

Library of Congress Control Number: 2012948962

Printed by Bookmasters Inc.
Ashland, Ohio

St. Joseph's Media

P. O. Box 186	P.O. Box 220208
Wayne, Michigan	Newhall, California
48184-0186	91322-0208

Acknowledgements

Special thanks to Paula Storm, BA, MILS for obtaining reference books and for her help in typing the manuscript, to Amanda Diehl for the unique and interesting cover design and to Fr. Gerard McKee, CMRI for proofreading the work.

Special thanks also to the students of St. Joseph's School who assisted with compiling practical vocabulary lists and for typing and helping compose exercises: Carolyn Cichos, Katelyn Cichos, Tyler Neumann, Luke Sabella, Olivia Sabella, Edmund Sentman, Richard Sentman, William Sentman, Michelle Tibai and Monica Tibai. Thanks also to Megan and Martha Tibai for their assistance.

This book is fun and easy to follow. Vocabulary revolves around practical aspects of daily life, not Roman soldiers and battles. Important words that need to be memorized are marked with an asterisk.*

A second book will be released soon that will explain other verb tenses, assist you in translating and give you a strong foundation in Latin.

Latin Alive

There are two types of Latin: classical and ecclesiastical. Classical is the Roman form used in legal documents, medicine and science. Ecclesiastical Latin, used by the Catholic Church for the Mass, sacraments, blessings, moral and dogmatic theology and Canon Law, often employs accent marks in place of long marks. The two differ in pronunciation of the letters **v** and **ae**. A Classical Latin **v** is pronounced like **w** and **ae** is pronounced like long **i**. Ecclesiastical Latin pronounces the letter **v** like **v** and **ae** like long **a**. Latin has been used for over 2,500 years.

An Amazing Language

Latin originated in the sixth century BC while the Latin Mass dates to 150 AD. The Catholic Church in Western Europe adopted Latin for the liturgy in 380 AD and the Latin Canon of the Mass was completed by 399 AD. Traditional Catholics still use Latin in the Mass, Divine Office and ritual.

St. Augustine of Canterbury (597 AD) and William the Conqueror (1066 AD) brought many Latin words to Britain that were assimilated into English. Nearly 80% of English words are of Latin origin, so memorization will be easy. Some words are exact; others are easily guessed or differ by just one or two letters.

Between the seventh and eight centuries Latin ceased to be a spoken language as it was transformed into Spanish, French, Italian, Portuguese and Romanian. This preserved the exact meaning of words and gave Latin its unchangeable nature. Amazingly, even after two millenia of use, it is very much alive today.

Scholars have used Latin for over a thousand years. Practical uses include the fields of medicine (prescriptions are written in Latin), law (many legal terms are in Latin) and science (plants and animals have a Latin or Greek name).

This book will increase your vocabulary, improve your diction and help you find the meaning of words from their Latin derivatives. Most words in the vocabulary lists are used in everyday language making *Latin Alive*. Exercises given in the back of the book will assist you to achieve a working use of the language.

Latin Pronunciation

In Latin, each vowel and consonant is pronounced separately with the following exceptions: **ae, ei, oe**; **ch, gn, ph** and **th**.

Latin consonants: **B D F K L M N P Q V X** sound the same as English. Others differ.

Consonants

c + ae, e, i, oe, y = **ch** + **vowel**

caelis (**chay** lees) a**ce**tum (ah **chay** toom) sacrifi**ci**um (sock rah fee **chee** oom) **co**eli (**chay** lee)

cc = tch e**cc**e (et **chay**)

ch = k (h is silent) **ch**erubim (**k**are oo bim)

g is hard lin**g**ua (leen **g**wah), but soft before ae, e, i, oe, y. **g**enetrix (**j**en ay treekx)

gn = ny (like canyon) a**gn**us (a **ny**oos)

h is silent In the words mi**h**i (me **k**ey) and ni**h**il (nee **k**eal) **h** is pronounced like **k**.

j = y **J**èsus (**Y**é soos) Some books replace **j** with **i** Iesus.

ph = f **ph**ilosophia (**f**e lo so fee ah)

qu = kw **qu**ì a (**kwee** ah)

r = slightly held pu**r**itas (pù**rr** **r**e tas)

sc = sh a**sc**endit (ah **sh**en deet)

th = t (h is silent) **th**rones pronounced (t**r**ò**w** nez)

ti + **vowel** = cé + vowel ora**ti**onem (oh rot **tsee** oh nem)

v is sometimes used as both the vowel **u** and the consonant **v**.

x = ks pa**x** (pah**kx**)

z = dz **z**i**z**ania (**dz**ee **dz**a ne ah)

Consonants are usually divided in pronunciation except ch, ph and th.

pa/ti/en/ti/ae (pah tsee en tsee ay)   Cher/u/bim (care oo bim)

Vowels

a = short a   mater (**mah** tare)
e = á   Deus (**Day** oos)
i = é   fìlia (**fee lee** ah)
o = ó   dominus (**dough** me noos)
u = short oo   cornu (cor **new**)
y = é   collyrida (coal **lee** ree da)

Dipthongs

vowel combinations that produce one sound
ae, oe = á aquae (a qw**á**) coeli (ch**á** lee)
two sounds quickly combined in one syllable
au = ow audi (**ow** dee)
ay = áá Raymundus (r**áá** moon duus)
two sounds said quickly in two syllables

ai = í é	**ait**	(**í** e**at**)
ei = á é	**rei**	(ray **é**)
eu = á oo	**euge**	(**á oo** já)
ou = oo ow	**prout**	(proo **out**)
ui = oo é	**tui**	(too **é**)

Nouns

persons, places, things

For example: e.g. (exemplo gratia) Deus (God), Maria (Mary), Roma (Rome), canis (dog), feles (cat), arbor (tree) and (et) saxum (rock).

Latin does not have words for the articles **a**, **an** and **the**. These articles are added to nouns in translation as needed (ad libitum).

Declensions

Nouns are listed in groups called declensions.

The **first declension** is feminine.

The **second declension** is masculine.

The **second declension neuter** is exactly like **2ⁿᵈ** masculine except:

> nominative and accusative singular are **um**.
>
> nominative and accusative plural are **a**.

The **third declension** is masculine and feminine.

The **third declension neuter** is exactly like **3ʳᵈ** m/f except:

> nominative and accusative singular are the same.
>
> nominative and accusative plural are **a**.

The **fourth declension** is masculine.

Fourth declension neuter uses **u** for nom, acc, abl and dat singular.

> nominative and accusative plural are **ua**.

The **fifth declension** is feminine.

Gender

Although declensions are given a **gender** (**m**, **f**, **n**), there are exceptions. The gender of a noun allows an adjective to match the noun it modifies. It is gender neutral (not exact).

Cases of Nouns

The use and meaning of a noun is determined by its **case**:

vocative, **nominative**, **accusative**, **ablative**, **dative**, **genitive**

Vocative   Direct Address (from the Latin *voco:* to call)

Nominative Subject of the Sentence (from the Latin *nomen:* name)

Accusative Direct Object or Object of Prepositions that take the Acc. case

Ablative   Object of a Preposition that takes the Abl. case

Dative   Indirect Object (to, for) (from the Latin *dare:* to give)

Genitive   Possessive (of) ('s)

Vocative Case

Vocative is taken from the verb "voco"—to call and is only used in direct address.   Second declension nouns become vocative by replacing the nominative **us** with **e**. A second declension noun ending in **ius** is made vocative by replacing **ius** with **í**.   Other declensions use the nominative singular or plural forms for the vocative case.

Dominus becomes Domine.   Domine, exaudi orationem meam.

Lord! hear my prayer.

Filius becomes Filí.   Filí, veni nunc!   Son, come now!

Example of the vocative case from the January 25th Divine Office:

Sancte Paule Apostole... St. Paul the Apostle...

First Declension

feminine

	Singular	Plural	
nominative	a	ae	subject of sentence
accusative	am	ás	direct object
ablative	á	ís	object of preposition
dative	ae	ís	indirect object (to, for)
genitive	ae	árum	possessive (of) ('s)

The girl went for a time to the villa with her cousin to see Mary's boat.

nominative   dative   accusative   ablative   genitive acc.

Puella tempori ad villam cum consobriná suá vidére naviculam Mariae venit.

nominative dative   accusative   ablative   accusative genitive

Declining a First Declension Noun

	Singular	Plural	S	P
nom	puella	puellae	girl	girls
acc	puellam	puellás	girl	girls
abl	puellá	puellís	with (by) the girl	with (by) the girl(s)
dat	puellae	puellís	to (for) the girl	to (for) the girls
gen	puellae	puellárum	girl's	girls'

Noun endings are color coded to help you better understand their useage.

Second Declension

masculine

	Singular	Plural	
nominative	**us**	**í**	subject of sentence
accusative	**um**	**ós**	direct object
ablative	**ó**	**ís**	object of preposition
dative	**ó**	**ís**	indirect object (to, for)
genitive	**í**	**órum**	possessive (of) ('s)

A **young man** went **to the school with his friend** to retrieve **Peter's books**.
        nominative   **accusative**   **ablative**   **genitive acc.**

Adolescentus ad scholam cum amicó ejus venit **Petrí librem** inveníre.
        nominative   **accusative**   **ablative**   **genitive accusative**

I confess **to Almighty God**.   Confiteor **Deó Omnipotentí**.
nominative   **dative**   **dative**

Declining a Second Declension Noun

	Singular	Plural	S	P
nom	**filius**	**filií**	son	sons
acc	**filium**	**filiós**	son	sons
abl	**filió**	**filiís**	with (by) the son	with (by) the sons
dat	**filió**	**filiís**	to (for) the son	to (for) the son
gen	**filií**	**filiórum**	son's	sons'

Some second declension nouns end in **r**: ager, puer and vir. The nominative is the stem to which second declension endings are added:

ager, agrum, agró, agó, agrí...

Second Declension Neuter

	Singular	Plural	
nominative	um	a	subject of sentence
accusative	um	a	direct object
ablative	ó	ís	object of preposition
dative	ó	ís	indirect object (to, for)
genitive	í	órum	possessive (of) ('s)

Horses ate the apples under the fruit tree.
nominative   accusative   ablative

Equi mala sub pomó manducavérunt.
nom.   acc.   ablative

Declining a Second Declension Neuter Noun

	Singular	Plural	S	P
nom	malum	mala	apple	apples
acc	malum	mala	apple	apples
abl	maló	malís	with (by) the apple	with (by) the apples
dat	maló	malís	to (for) the apple	to (for) the apples
gen	malí	malórum	apple's	apples'

Third Declension

masculine and feminine

	Singular	Plural	
nominative	varies	és	subject of the sentence
accusative	em	és	direct object
ablative	e	ibus	object of preposition
dative	í	ibus	indirect object (to, for)
genitive	is	um (ium)	possessive (of) ('s)

The genitive plural ending **ium** is used when the word stem ends in two consonants: mons, mo**nt**is (m) mountain and when a noun has the same number of syllables in its nominative and genitive forms: **feles**, **felis** (f) cat   **canis**, **canis** (m/f) dog.

Third Declension Neuter

	Singular	Plural	
nominative	varies	a	subject of the sentence
accusative	same as nominative	a	direct object
ablative	e	ibus	object of preposition
dative	í	ibus	indirect object (to, for)
genitive	is	um	possessive (of) ('s)

Fourth Declension

masculine

	Singular	Plural	
nominative	us	ús	subject of the sentence
accusative	um	ús	direct object
ablative	ú	ibus	object of preposition
dative	uí	ibus	indirect object (to, for)
genitive	ús	uum	possessive (of) ('s)

Some fourth declension nouns are feminine: **domus**, **ús** (f) house **manus**, **ús** (f) hand

Fourth Declension Neuter

	Singular	Plural	
nominative	ú	ua	subject of the sentence
accusative	ú	ua	direct object
ablative	ú	ibus	object of preposition
dative	ú	ibus	indirect object (to, for)
genitive	ús	uum	possessive (of) ('s)

Fifth Declension

feminine

	Singular	Plural	
nominative	és	és	subject of the sentence
accusative	em	és	direct object
ablative	é	ébus	object of preposition
dative	eí	ébus	indirect object (to, for)
genitive	eí	érum	possessive (of) ('s)

Noun Forms

Nouns in a Latin sentence have specific endings.

- A **subject** uses the **nominative** case.
- A **direct object** uses the **accusative** case.
- An **object of preposition** is in either the **accusative or ablative** case depending on the preposition used.
- An **indirect object** uses the **dative** case.
- **Possession** is shown by using the **genitive** case.
- The **vocative** case is used for **direct address**.

Placement

- The **subject** is usually the first word in the sentence.
- The **indirect object** usually follows the subject.
- The **direct object** usually follows the indirect object.
- The **object of preposition** follows the direct object.
- **Adjectives** usually follow nouns and agree with nouns in gender, number and case.
- **Adverbs** and **conjunctions** are used as needed.
- The **verb** is usually the last word in the sentence.

Word Construction

A noun may be changed from masculine to feminine or visa versa by replacing the masculine ending **us** with **a**: Julius, Julia.

Adjectives may be transformed into nouns when necessary: medicus, a, um is an adjective that means medical, healing.

medicus, **í** is a second declension noun: male physician
medica, **ae** is a first declension noun: female physician

Compound words may be constructed from a preposition and a verb: adduco.

ad (to) + **duco** (lead) = **adduco**: lead to

Prepositions

The word after a preposition will be in either the **accusative** or **ablative** case.

Nouns following these prepositions take the **accusative case**:

ad*	to, towards
adversus	against
ante*	before
apud	to, before, with
circum*	around
contra*	against
erga	towards, for, with
extra*	outside, beyond
in*	into
inter*	between
intra*	within
ob	for, in consideration of
penes	with, within
per*	through
post*	after
propter*	for, because of
secundum*	according to
supra*	over, upon
trans*	through, across
ultra*	beyond, farther, besides

Nouns following these prepositions take the **ablative case**:

a* (before consonants):	by, away from
ab* (before vowels):	by, away from
absque	without, but for
coram*	in the presence of
cum*	with
de*	down from, concerning
e* (before consonants):	out of, from
ex* (before vowels):	out of, from
in*	in or on
prae*	before
pro*	for, through, in behalf of
sine*	without
sub*	under

* memorize these commonly used prepositions

Understanding Vocabulary Lists

Vocabulary lists give nominative and genitive forms. The noun stem is taken from the nominative form for 1st, 2nd, 4th and 5th declension nouns. The stem of a 3rd declension noun is taken from the genitive form minus the **is**.

		nominative	genitive
First Declension	puella, puellae (f) girl	a	ae
Second Declension	equus, equí (m)	us	í
(ending in the letter r)	puer, puerí (m) boy	r	í
Second Declension Neuter	auxilium, ií (n) help	um	í
Third Declension	canis, canis (m/f) dog	varies	is
Third Declension Neuter	caput, capitis (n): head	varies	is
Fourth Declension	portus, portús (m)	us	ús
Fourth Declension Neuter	cornú, cornús (n)	ú	ús
Fifth Declension	rés, reí (f)	és	eí

Finding Noun Stems

Declension	Vocabulary Listing	Stem
	(nominative and genitive forms and gender)	
First	puella, ae (f)	puell
Second	equus, equí (m)	equ
	puer, puerí (m)	puer
Second Neuter	auxilium, auxilií (n)	auxili
Third	canis, canis (m/f)	can
Third Neuter	caput, capitis (n)	capit
Fourth	portus, portús (m)	port
Fourth Neuter	cornú, cornús (n)	corn
Fifth	rés, reí (f)	re

Accent Marks for Nouns

Accent marks facilitate the reading of Latin. Classical Latin utilizes long marks over vowels while Ecclesiastical Latin uses acute accent.

Memorize accent marks given on the declension charts especially the ablative form of the First Declension. This is the only way to distinguish the nominative and ablative forms. Also memorize vocabulary that is marked with an asterisk.*

Nouns
Anatomy Anatomia

*aetas, aetatis (f) age	3rd declension
*auris, auris (f) ear	3rd
*brachium, brachii (n) arm	2nd n
calvaria, calvariae (f) skull	1st
capillus, capilli (m) hair	2nd
*caput, capitis (n) head	3rd n
cauda, caudae (f) tail	1st
cerebrum, cerebri (n) brain	2nd n
collum, colli (n) neck	2nd n
*cor, cordis (n) heart	3rd n
*corpus, corporis (n) body	3rd n
*dens, dentis (m) tooth	3rd
*digitus, digiti (m) finger, toe	2nd
*faciés, faciei (f) face, form	5th
genu, genús (n) knee	4th n
guttur, gutturis (n) throat	3rd n
humerus, humeri (m) shoulder	2nd
labium, labii (n) lip	2nd n
*lingua, linguae (f) tongue, language	1st
*manús, manús (f) hand	4th
maxilla, maxillae (f) jaw	1st
membrum, membri (n) member, limb	2nd n
*mens, mentis (f) mind	3rd
*nasus, nasús (m) nose	4th

*oculus, oculí (m) eye	2nd
*ós, óris (n) mouth, beak	3rd n
*os, ossis (n) bone	3rd n
ossa, ossórum (n) skeleton	2nd n pl
*pes, pedis (m) foot	3rd
*sanguis, sanguinis (m) blood	3rd
scapulae, scapulárum (f) shoulders, back	1st pl
venter, ventris (m) stomach, womb	3rd

Animals Animalia

accipiter, accipitris (m) hawk	3rd
*agnus, agní (m) lamb	2nd
*animal, animalis (n) animal	3rd n
*aquila, aquilae (f) eagle	1st
aranea, araneae (f) spider	1st
aries, arietis (m) ram	3rd
apis, apis (f) bee	3rd
*avis, avis (f) bird	3rd
*bos, bovis (m/f) ox, cow	3rd
cancer, cancerí (m) crab	2nd
*canis, canis (m/f) dog	3rd
caper, caperí (m) goat	2nd
capra, caprae (f) goat	1st
*cervus, cerví (m) deer, buck	2nd
*cetus, cetí (m) whale	2nd
cimex, cimicis (m) bug, insect	3rd
*columba, columbae (f) dove	1st
corvus, corví (m) raven	2nd
crocodilus, crocodilí (m) crocodile	2nd
cuniculus, cuniculí (m) rabbit	2nd
elephas, elephantis (m) elephant	3rd
*equus, equí (m) horse	2nd
*feles, felis (f) cat	3rd
*grex, gregis (m) flock, herd, swarm	3rd
lacerta, lacertae (f) lizard	1st
*leo, leonis (m) lion	3rd
*lea, leae (f) lioness	1st

*gallus, gallí (m) rooster — 2nd

*gallina, gallinae (f) hen — 1st

*lupus, lupí (m) wolf — 2nd

*lupa, lupae (f) wolf — 1st

mulus, mulí (m) mule — 2nd

*mus, muris (m/f) mouse, rat — 3rd

*musca, muscae (f) fly — 1st

*pecus, pecoris (n) cattle, herd, flock — 3rd n

pecus, pecudis (f) animal — 3rd

*piscis, piscis (m) fish — 3rd

*porca, porcae (f) sow — 1st

*porcus, porcí (m) pig — 2nd

rana, ranae (f) frog — 1st

rubeta, rubetae (f) toad — 1st

sciurus, sciurí (m) squirrel — 2nd

*serpens, serpentis (f) snake — 3rd

*taurus, taurí (m) bull — 2nd

*tigris, tigris (m/f) tiger — 3rd

*tinea, tineae (f) moth, bookworm — 1st

*ursus, ursí (m) bear — 2nd

*ursa, ursae (f) bear — 1st

*vaca, vacae (f) cow — 1st

*volpes, volpis (f) fox — 3rd

volpes marina (f) shark — 3rd 1st

*volucris, volucris (f) bird, fowl — 3rd

locus animaliárum zoo — 2nd 1st pl

Building Aedificium

*academia, ae (f) academy, college — 1st

*aedificium, aedificií or í (n) building — 2nd n

*atrium, atrií (n) court, house, room — 2nd n

*casa, casae (f) house — 1st

*copia, copiae (f) store — 1st

*culina, culinae (f) kitchen — 1st

*domus, domí (m) home — 2nd

*domus, domús (m) home — 4th

*ecclesia, ecclesiae (f) church — 1st

*fenestra, fenestrae (f) window   1st

*fons, fontis (m) font, fountain   3rd

fornax, fornacis (f) oven, furnace   3rd

forum, forí (n) shopping center, marketplace   2nd n

*furnus, furní (m) oven   2nd

fundamentum, fundamentí (n) foundation   2nd n

*gradus, gradús (m) step, pace, walk   4th

*habitaculum, habituculí (n) dwelling   2nd n

*horreum, horreí (n) barn, shed, garage   2nd n

*janua, janae (f) door   1st

ingressus, ingressús (m) entrance   4th

*latrina, latrinae (f) restroom   1st

latibulum, latibulí (n) hiding place   2nd n

limen, liminis (n) threshold   3rd n

*locus, locí (m) place, room   2nd

*murus, murí (m) wall   2nd

*ostium, ostií or í (n) door, entrance   2nd n

*porta, portae (f) gate   1st

*schola, scholae (f) school, class   1st

spatium, spatií (or í) (n) space, room   2nd n

*taberna, tabernae (f) store, shop   1st

taberna medicina, ae, ae (f) drugstore   1st

*tectum, tectí (n) roof   2nd n

valetudinarium, -ií (n) hospital   2nd n

*villa, villae (f) country house, farm, villa   1st

Characterisics Proprietates

*aegritudo, aegritudinis (f) sickness   3rd

*amicitia, amicitiae (f) friendship   1st

*causa, causae (f) cause, case, reason   1st

*celeritas, celeritatis (f) speed   3rd

*cogitio, cogitionis (f) thinking   3rd

commotio, commotionis (f) emotion   3rd

*cura, curae (f) care, concern   1st

*décor, decoris (m) beauty, elegance   3rd

*dignitas, dignitatis (f) dignity, merit   3rd

*dolor, doloris (m) sorrow, dolor   3rd

*felicitas, felicitatis (f) happiness	3rd
*intellectus, intellectús (m) intellect	4th
*ira, irae (f) wrath, anger	1st
*monitio, monitionis (f) warning	3rd
naviatas, naviatatis (f) zeal, energy	3rd
*odium, odií (n) hatred	2nd n
proprietas, proprietatis (f) ownership	3rd
*salus, salutis (f) salvation, health	3rd
*sententia, ae (f) feeling, opinion	1st
*timor, timoris (m) fear	3rd
*voluntas, voluntatis (f) will, wish	3rd

Clothing Vestis

bracae, bracárum (f) pants	1st pl
*calceatus, calceatí (m) shoe, sandal	2nd
*cingulum, cingulí (n) belt, sash	2nd n
habitus, habitús (m) dress, habit	4th
instita, institae (f) skirt	1st
pallium, pallií (n) cloak	2nd n
pilleus, pilleí (m) hat, cap	2nd
solea, soleae (f) sandal	1st
subucula, ae (f) shirt, blouse, vest	1st
*tunica, ae (f) tunic	1st
*vestimentum, í (n) clothing	2nd n
*vestis, vestis (f) clothing	3rd

Food Cibus

acetum, acetí (n) vinegar	2nd n
apium, apií (f) parsley	2nd n
ariena, arienae (f) banana	1st
*aqua, aquae (f) water	1st
avenae, avenarum (f) oats	1st pl
bacca, baccae (f) berry	1st
bubula, bubulae (f) beef	1st
bulbus, bulbí (m) onion	2nd
*butyrum, butyrí (n) butter	2nd n
canis caldus hot dog	

*carnis, carnis (f) meat	3rd
*caseum, casei (n) cheese	2nd n
cerasum, cerasi (n) cherry	2nd n
*chocolatum, chocolati (n) chocolate	2nd n
coffea Arabica, ae, ae (f) coffee	1st
*collyrida, collyridae (f) cake, pastry	1st
condimentum, condimenti (n) sauce	2nd n
*convivium, convivii (n) banquet, party	2nd n
*crema, cremae (f) cream	1st
*crustulum, crustuli (n) pastry, cookie	2nd n
crustum, crusti (n) pie	2nd n
*esca, escae (f) food, dish, bait	1st
*farina, farinae (f) flour	1st
malum mendicum, mali mendici (n) lemon	2nd n 2nd n
*fructus, fructús (m) fruit, produce	4th
*frumentum, i (n) cereal, grain, corn	2nd n
fungus, fungi (m) mushroom	2nd
*lac, lactis (n) milk	3rd n
lagadum, lagadi (n) pancake	2nd n
lardum, lardi (n) bacon, fat, lard	2nd n
flos lactis glacies ice cream	
flos, floris (m) lac, lactis (m) glacies, ei (f)	
gummis salvivaia chewing gum	3rd 1st
malum, mali (n) apple	2nd n
malum aurantium, i, i (n) orange	2nd n
*mel, mellis (n) honey	3rd n
menta, mentae (f) mint	1st
muria, muriae (f) pickle	1st
nux, nucis (f) nut	3rd
nitrum, nitri (n) soda (pop)	2nd n
oliva, olivae (f) olive	1st
olivum, olivi (n) olive oil	2nd n
*ovum, ovi (n) egg	2nd n
*panis, panis (m) bread	3rd
perna, pernae (f) ham	1st
pinea, pineae (f) pineapple	1st
piper, piperis (n) pepper	3rd n
pirum, piri (n) pear	2nd n

polenta, polentae (f) barley	1st
*****pomum, pomí** (n) fruit	2nd n
pomus, pomí (m) fruit tree	2nd
*****potus, potús** (m) drink	4th
saccharum crystallinum candy	2nd n pl 3rd pl
*****sal, salis** (m) salt	3rd
scilla, scillae (f) shrimp	1st
*****semen, seminis** (n) seed	3rd n
sinapis, sinapis (f) mustard	3rd
sucus, sucí (m) juice	3rd
*****triticum, tritici** (n) wheat	2nd n
*****uva, uvae** (f) grape	1st
*****vinum, viní** (n) wine	2nd n
jentaculum, jentaculí (n) breakfast	2nd n
prandium, prandií (n) lunch, brunch	2nd n
*****cena, cenae** (f) dinner	1st

Materials Materiae

arena, arenae (f) sand	1st
*****argentum, argentí** (n) silver	2nd n
*****aurum, aurí** (n) gold	2nd n
carbo, carbonis (m) coal	3rd
cuprum, cuprí (n) copper	2nd n
*****ferrum, ferrí** (n) iron	2nd n
funis, funis (m) rope	3rd
*****gemma, gemmae** (f) gem, jewel	1st
*****lignum, ligní** (n) wood	2nd n
*****margarita, margaritae** (f) pearl	1st
*****materia, materiae** (f) material, timber	1st
mettalum, mettalí (n) metal	2nd n
orichacum, orichací (n) brass	2nd n
*****plumbum, plumbí** (n) lead	2nd n
sal gemma, salis gemmae rock salt	3rd 1st
*****saxum, í** (n) stone, rock	2nd n

Measurement Mensura

*****duodecim**	dozen
sexarius, sexarií (m)	pint
duo sexarií	quart
congius, congií (m)	gallon
mensura, mensurae (f)	measurement

Months Menses

Januarius	January
Februarius	February
Martius	March
Aprilis	April
Maius	May
Junius	June
Julius	July
Augustus	August
September, Septembris	September
October, Octobris	October
November, Novembris	November
December, Decembris	December

Military Terms Verba Militiae

aciés, **acieí** (f) battleline, battle array	5th
aggeris, **aggeris** (m) mound, rampart	3rd
arma, **armórum** (n) armor	2nd n pl
*****bellum**, **bellí** (n) war	2nd n
caedes, **caedis** (f) slaughter	3rd
carcer, **carceris** (m) prison	3rd
*****castra**, **castrórum** (n) military camp	2nd n pl
*****clamor**, **clamoris** (m) cry, shout, call	3rd
clipeus, **clipeí** (m) round shield	2nd
*****concilium**, **concilií** (m) council	2nd n
*****cornu**, **cornús** (n) horn	4th n
ductus, **ductí** (m) leadership	2nd
edictum, **edictí** (n) decree, edict	2nd n
exercitus, **exercitús** (m) army, flock	3rd
exitium, **exitií** or **exití** (n) destruction	2nd n
*****finis**, **finis** (m) border, end	3rd
fovea, **foveae** (f) ditch, pit	1st
*****galea**, **galae** (f) helmet	1st
*****gladius**, **gladií** (m) sword	2nd
pila, **pilae** (f) spear	1st
*****imperium**, **ií** (n) dominion, command	2nd n
*****impetus**, **impetús** (m) attack, force	4th
latus, **lateris** (n) side, flank	3rd n
*****legio**, **legionis** (f) legion	3rd

*militia, militiae (f) army, militia — 1st

munitio, munitionis (f) defenses — 3rd

naufragium, naufragií (n) shipwreck — 2nd n

naufragius, naufragií (n) boatman — 2nd

*navis, navis (f) ship, boat — 3rd

*ordo, ordinis (m) order, rank, class — 3rd

pelta, peltae (f) light shield — 1st

*periculum, periculí (n) danger — 2nd n

*poena, poenae (f) penalty, punishment — 1st

*proelium, proelii (n) battle — 2nd n

*regnum, regní (n) kingdom, authority — 2nd n

*sagitta, sagittae (f) arrow — 1st

*scutum, scutí (n) shield — 2nd n

sica, sicae (f) dagger — 1st

telum, telí (n) javelin, missile — 2nd n

tormentum, tormentí (n) cannon — 2nd n

venenum, venení (n) poison — 2nd n

Musical Instuments
Instrumentae Musicae

*cantus, cantús (m) song — 4th

*cithara, citharae (f) zither, lute — 1st

instrumentum, í (n) instrument, tool — 2nd n

*lyra, lyrae (f) harp — 1st

musicus, a, um (adj) musical — 2nd 1st 2nd n

*tuba, tubae (f) trumpet — 1st

People Populí

*adolescens, entis (m/f) young man, young woman — 3rd

*agricola, agricolae (m) farmer — 1st

*amica, amicae (f) friend — 1st

*amicus, amicí (m) friend — 2nd

amita, amitae (f) aunt (father's side) — 2nd

*ancilla, ancillae (f) handmaid — 1st

avia, aviae (f) grandmother — 1st

avunculus, avunculí (m) uncle — 2nd

avus, aví (m) grandfather — 2nd

*civis, civis (m/f) citizen — 3rd

consobrinus, consobriní (m) cousin — 2nd

consobrina, consobrinae (f) cousin   1st

*__discipulus, discipulí__ (m) student, pupil   2nd

*__discipula, discipulae__ (f) student, pupil   1st

*__doctor, doctoris__ (m) doctor, teacher   3rd

*__domina, dominae__ (f) lady   1st

*__dominus, dominí__ (m) lord   2nd

*__dux, ducis__ (m/f) leader   3rd

*__episcopus, episcopí__ (m) bishop   2nd

faber, fabrí (m) craftsman   2nd

*__famulus, famulí__ (m) servant   2nd

*__famula, famulae__ (f) servant   1st

*__femina, feminae__ (f) female, woman   1st

*__filia, filiae__ (f) daughter   1st

*__filius, filií__ (m) son   2nd

*__frater, fratris__ (m) brother, friar   3rd

geminus, geminí (m) twin   2nd

*__genetrix, genetricis__ (f) mother   3rd

*__gens, gentis__ (f) tribe, people, clan   3rd

*__homo, hominis__ (m) man   3rd

*__inimicus, inimicí__ (m) enemy   2nd

*__invicem__ one another   indeclinable

*__judex, judicis__ (m) judge   3rd

*__juventa, juventae__ (f) youth   1st

*__magister, magistrí__ (m) teacher, master   2nd

marita, maritae (f) married woman   1st

maritus, marití (m) married man   2nd

*__mater, matris__ (f) mother   3rd

matertera, ae (f) aunt (mother's side)   1st

*__medicus, medicí__ (m) doctor   2nd

*__miles, milites__ (m) soldier   3rd

*__mulier, mulieris__ (f) woman, lady   3rd

*__nauta, nautae__ (m) sailor   1st

*__nemo, neminis__ (n) no one   3rd n

*__papa, papae__ (m) pope   1st

*__parens, parentis__ (m/f) parents   3rd

parochus, í (m) parish priest, pastor   2nd

*__pastor, pastoris__ (m) shepherd, pastor   3rd

*__pater, patris__ (m) father   3rd

patrinus, patriní (m) sponsor   2nd

patriarcha, patriarchae (m) patriarch   1st

peritus, periti (m) expert, advisor 2nd
pirata, piratae (m) pirate 1st
*****populus, populi** (m) people 2nd
*****presbyter, presbyteri** (m) priest, elder 2nd
*****princeps, principis** (m) ruler 3rd
*****proles, prolis** (f) offspring 3rd
*****puella** (f) girl 1st
*****puer, pueri** (m) boy 2nd
*****regina, reginae** (f) queen 1st
regulus filia, reguli filiae (f) princess 2nd 1st
regulus filius, reguli filii (m) prince 2nd
*****rex, regis** (m) king 3rd
*****senex, senis** (m, f) old man, old woman 3rd
*****soror, sororis** (f) sister 3rd
*****uxor, uxoris** (f) wife 3rd
vicina, vicinae (f) neighbor 1st
vicinus, vicini (m) neighbor 2nd
*****victima, victimae** (f) victim 1st
*****vidua, vidae** (f) widow 1st
*****vir, viri** (m) man 2nd
*****virgo, virginis** (f) virgin, maiden 3rd

Plants Plantae

bellis, bellis (f) daisy 3rd
bulbus, bulbi (m) bulb 2nd
*****cedrus, cedri** (m) cedar 2nd
faenum, faeni (m) hay 2nd n
*****flos, floris** (m) flower, bud 3rd
folium, folii or **foli** (n) leaf 2nd n
frondes, frondium (n) foliage 3rd n pl
frutex, -icis (m) bush (comic): blockhead 3rd
*****herba, herbae** (f) herb 1st
hyacinthus, hyacinthi (m) hyacinth 2nd
*****lilium, lilii** or **lili** (n) lily 2nd n
narcissus, narcissi (m) daffodil 2nd
*****planta, plantae** (f) plant 1st
*****rosa, rosae** (f) rose 1st
*****spina, spinae** (f) thorn 1st
trifolium, trifolii (n) clover 2nd n
*****zizania, zizaniorum** (n) weeds, cockle 2nd n pl

Religious Words Verba Religiosae

*adventus, adventí (m) coming, arrival	2nd
*aeternitas, -atis (f) eternity, eternal life	3rd
*altare, altaris (n) altar	3rd n
*angelus, angelí (m) angel	2nd
*anima, animae (f) soul	1st
*beatitudo, beatitudinis (f) happiness	3rd
*benedictio, benedictionis (f) blessing	3rd
*calix, calicis (m) chalice, cup	3rd
*capella, capellae (f) chapel	1st
*Christus, Christí (m) Christ	2nd
*chorus, chorí (m) choir	2nd
*culpa, culpae (f) fault, blame	1st
*crux, crucis (f) cross	3rd
*Deus, Deí (m) God	2nd
*divinitas, divinitatis divinity	3rd
divus, diví (m) saint	2nd
*erratum, erratí (n) error, mistake	2nd n
*festum, festí (n) feast, festival	2nd n
*hostia, hostiae (f) host, victim, sacrifice	1st
*indulgentia, ae (f) indulgence, pardon	1st
*infer(n)us, infer(n)í (m) hell	2nd
*jejunium, jejunií or í (n) fasting, fast	2nd n
*Jesus, ù[1] (m) Jesus	4th
*Missa, Missae (f) Mass	1st
*nefas sin, wrong, unlawful	indecl
*oratio, orationis (f) prayer	3rd
*Paradisus, í (m) Paradise, Heaven	2nd
*parochus, parochí (m) parish	2nd
*peccatum, peccatí (n) sin	2nd n
preceptum, preceptí (n) rule, precept	2nd n
*passio, passionis (f) suffering, passion	3rd
*prex, precis (f) prayer	3rd
*reliquiae, árum (f) remains, relics	1st pl
*sacerdos, sacerdotis (m) priest	3rd
*sancta, sanctae (f) saint	1st
*sanctitas, -atis (f) sanctity, holiness	3rd

---

[1] nom. Jesus acc. Jesum abl. Jesù dat. Jesù gen. Jesù voc. Jesù

*sanctus, sanctí (m) saint   2nd
*spiritus, -ús (f) spirit, ghost, breath   4th
*tabernaculum, í (n) tabernacle, tent   2nd n
*trinitas, trinitatis (f) trinity   3rd
*verbum, verbí (n) word   2nd n
*veritas, veritatis (f) truth   3rd

Shapes Formae

circulus, circulí (m) circle, hoop   2nd
gyrus, gyrí (m) circle, ring, oval   2nd
ovatus, ovatí (m) oval   2nd
quadrum, quadrí (n) square   2nd n
species, specieí (f) shape, sight, view   5th
triangulum, trianguli (n) triangle   2nd n

Things Res

*annulus, annulí (m) ring   2nd
arca, arcae (f) box   1st
bulla, bullae (f) papal document   1st
caminus, caminí (m) chimney   2nd
*catena, catenae (f) chain, fetter   1st
*cathedra, cathedrae (f) chair   1st
catillus, catillí (m) small dish   2nd
catinus, catiní (m) plate, pot   2nd
*cera, cerae (f) wax   1st
*clavis, clavis (f) key   3rd
*clavus, claví (m) nail   2nd
*conclave, conclavis (n) room   3rd n
*corona, coronae (f) crown   1st
*currus, currús (m) chariot, car   4th
*donum, doní (n) gift   2nd n
*horologium, horologií (n) clock   2nd n
*ignis, ignis (m) fire   3rd
*lacrima, lacrimae (f) tear   1st
*laqueus, laqueí (m) snare, trap, noose   2nd
lectus, lectí (m) bed, couch   2nd
*liber, librí (m) book   2nd
litterae, litterárum (f) literature   1st pl
lucerna, lucernae (f) lamp   1st
*lumen, luminis (n) lamp, light   3rd n

*mensa, mensae (f) table	1st
*pagina, paginae (f) page	1st
pannus, panní (m) cloth	2nd
*pecunia, pecuniae (f) money, property	1st
pelvis, pelvis (f) bucket, basin	3rd
*petra, petrae (f) rock	1st
*praemium, praemií (n) reward, prize	2nd n
poculum, poculí (n) cup, drink	2nd n
*pulvis, pulveris (m) dust, ashes	3rd
*rés, reí (f) thing, object, event	5th
saccus, saccí (m) bag	2nd
scopula, scopulae (f) brush	1st
*sedes, sedis (f) seat, throne	3rd
thalerus, thalerí (m) dollar	2nd
*vas, vasis (n) vessel, dish	3rd n
*via, viae (f) way, road, street	1st
vitrum, vitrí (n) glass	2nd n

Time Tempus

*aetas, aetatis (f) summer	3rd
*autumnus, autumní (m) autumn	2nd
*annus, anní (m) year	2nd
*diés, dieí (m) day	5th
*feria, feriae (f) day of the week	1st
*hebdomada, hebdomadae (f) week	1st
*hiems, hiemis (f) winter	3rd
mané in the morning	3rd abl
*mensis, mensis (m) month	3rd
ante meridiem morning a.m.	
post meridiem afternoon p.m.	
meridies, meridieí (f) noon	5th
*nox, noctis (f) night	3rd
prima luce early in the morning	
*tempus, temporis (m) time	3rd
*tempus vernum springtime	
*tenebrae, tenebrárum (f) (pl) darkness	1st
*vespera, vesperae (f) evening	1st
vespere in the evening	

Virtues Virtutes

*amor, amoris (m) love, affection	3rd
benevolentia, benevolentiae (f) benevolence	1st
benignitas, benignitatis (f) kindness	3rd
*caritas, caritatis (f) charity, love	3rd
*diligentia, diligentiae (f) dilligence	1st
dulcedo, dulcedinis (f) sweetness, goodness	3rd
*fidés, fideí (f) faith, trust	5th
fiducia, fiduciae (f) trust, confidence	1st
*fortitudo, fortitudinis (f) fortitude, strength	3rd
*gaudium, gaudií or í (n) joy, delight	2nd n
*humilitas, humilitatis (f) humility	3rd
*laetitia, laetitiae (f) happiness	1st
*justitia, justitiae (f) justice	1st
*mansuetudo, mansuetudis (f) mildness	3rd
*misericordia, misericordiae (f) mercy	1st
*modestia, modestiae (f) modesty, chastity	1st
*patientia, patientiae (f) patience	1st
*pax, pacis (f) peace	3rd
*prudentia, prudentiae (f) prudence	1st
pudicitia, pudicitiae (f) modesty, purity	1st
*puritas, puritatis (f) purity	3rd
*robur, roboris (n) strength, power	3rd n
*spés, speí (f) hope, trust	5th
*virtus, virtutis (f) virtue, power	3rd

Weather Caelum

*caelum, caelí (n) sky, heaven, weather	2nd n
dilivium, dilivií (n) flood	2nd n
gelú, gelús (n) icy cold, frost	4th n
*glaciés, glacieí (f) ice	5th
grando, grandinis (f) hail	3rd
*nix, nivis (f) snow	3rd
*nubes, nubis (f) cloud	3rd
*pluvia, pluviae (f) rain	1st
procella, procellae (f) hurricane	1st
*tempestas, tempestatis (f) tempest	3rd
tonitrus, tonitrús (m) thunder	4th
*ventus, ventí (m) wind	2nd

The World Orbis

*abscondita, absconditae (f) hidden place	1st
*aer, aeris (m) air, sky, heaven	3rd
*ager, agerí (m) field	2nd
*campus, campí (m) field	2nd
cataracta, cataractae (f) waterfall	1st
*civitas, civitatis (f) city	3rd
*collis, collis (m) hill	3rd
desertum, desertí (n) desert, wilderness	2nd n
fluetum, flueti (n) stream	2nd n
*flumen, fluminis (n) river	3rd n
fovea, foveae (f) ditch, pit	1st
*hortus, hortí (m) garden	2nd
hortí, hortórum park	2nd pl
*lacus, lací (m) lake	2nd
*luna, lunae (f) moon	1st
*mare, maris (n) sea	3rd
*mons, montis (m) mountain	3rd
*mundus, mundí (m) world	2nd
*orbis, orbis (m) world	3rd
*orbis terrae, orbis terrarum	3rd 1st pl
earth, world, universe	
patria, patriae (f) country, native land,	1st
*portus, portús (m) port, harbor	4th
regio, regionis (f) country, region	3rd
*silva, silvae (f) forest, woods	1st
*sol, solis (m) sun	3rd
*stella, stellae (f) star	1st
*terra, terrae (f) land	1st
*urbs, urbis (f) city	3rd
*umbra, umbrae (f) shadow, shade, ghost	1st

And the Rest Et Cetera

abominatio, **onis** (f) loathing, aversion	3rd
*****adjutorium**, **adjutorií** (n) help, assistance	2nd n
analysis, **analysis** (f) analysis	3rd
calculus, **calculí** (m) stone, pebble	2nd
*****campana**, **campanae** (f) bell	1st
cista, **cistae** (f) box	1st
coetus, **coetús** (m) meeting	4th
*****convivium**, **convivií** (n) banquet	2nd n
detrimentum, **detrimentí** (n) loss, injury	2nd n
*****dimidium**, **dimidií** (m) half	2nd
distantia, **distantiae** (f) distance	1st
*****dormitio**, **dormitionis** (f) sleep	3rd
edictum, **edictí** (n) decree, edict	2nd n
effectus, **effectí** (m) effect	2nd
*****eleemosyna**, **eleemosynae** (f) alms	1st
*****error**, **erroris** (m) error	3rd
*****epistola (epistula)**, **ae** (f) letter	1st
*****fletus**, **fletús** (m) crying, (plural) tears	4th
*****gustus**, **gustí** (m) taste	2nd
*****hereditas**, **hereditatis** (f) inheritance	3rd
*****heres**, **heredis** (m) heir	3rd
*****hostis**, **hostis** (m/f) enemy	3rd
*****initium**, **initií** (n) beginning	2nd n
*****iter**, **inineris** (n) journey, trip	3rd n
*****jocus**, **jocí** (m) fun	2nd
*****languor**, **languoris** (m) infirmity, sickness	3rd
*****littera**, **ae** (f) letter, epistle	1st
*****majestas**, **majestatis** (f) dignity, majesty	3rd
*****macula**, **maculae** (f) spot, stain	1st
*****lux**, **lucis** (f) light	3rd
machina itere aereo destinata airplane	
*****mandatum**, **mandatí** (n) order, command	2nd n
*****materia**, **materiae** (f) matter, material	1st
medela, **medelae** (f) cure, remedy	1st
*****memoria**, **memoriae** (f) memory	1st
menda, **mendae** (f) fault, blemish	1st
*****mendacium**, **mendacií** (n) lie	2nd n
*****modus**, **modí** (m) way, manner	2nd

*monitus, monitús (m) warning	4th
*mors, mortis (f) death	3rd
mora, morae (f) delay	1st
*mos, moris (m) habit, custom	3rd
*nomen, nominis (n) name	3rd n
*natura, ae (f) nature	1st
*numisma, numismatis (n) coin	3rd n
*pignus, pignoris (n) pledge	3rd n
*ratio, rationis (f) reason, matter	3rd
*requiés, requieí (f) rest, repose	5th
*opus, operis (n) work, task	3rd n
*pars, partis (f) part, share, portion	3rd
*potentia, potentiae (f) power, might	1st
*pretium, pretií (n) worth, price, value	2nd n
quisquiliae, quisquiliárum (f) (pl) trash	1st pl
*scientia, scientiae (f) knowledge	1st
*scriptus, a, um composition, homework	4th pp of scribo
*sonus, soní (m) sound	2nd
*superbia, superbiae (f) pride	1st
*theausaurus, -í (m) treasure, storehouse	2nd
venia, veniae (f) pardon, forgiveness	1st
vis, vis (f) force, violence	3rd
*visio, visionis (f) vision	3rd
*vita, vitae (f) life	1st
*vox, vocis (f) voice	3rd
*vultus, vultús (m) face, expression	4th

Personal Pronouns

First Person Singular			Second Person Singular		
nominative	ego	I	tú	you	
accusative	mé	me	té	you	
ablative	mé	with me	té	with you	
dative	mihi	to (or for) me	tibi	to (or for) you	
genitive	meí	mine	tuí	yours	

First Person Plural			Second Person Plural		
nominative	nós	we	vós	you	
accusative	nós	us	vós	you	
ablative	nobís	with us	vobís	with you	
dative	nobís	to (or for) us	vobís	to (or for) you	
genitive	nostrí	our	vestrí	your	

Third Person Singular

	M		F		N	
nominative	is	he	ea	she	id	it
accusative	eum	him	eam	her	id	it
ablative	eó	with him	eá	with her	eó	with it
dative	eí	to or for him	eí	to or for her	eí	to (or for) it
genitive	ejus	his	ejus	her	ejus	its

Third Person Plural

	M	F	N	
nominative	eí	eae	ea	they
accusative	eós	eás	ea	them
ablative	eís	eís	eís	with them
dative	eís	eís	eís	to (or for) them
genitive	eórum	eárum	eórum	their

Demonstrative Adjectives and Pronouns

hic   haec   hoc

Singular

	M	F	N	
nom.	hic	haec	hoc	this
acc.	hunc	hanc	hoc	this
abl.	hóc	hác	hóc	with (by) this
dat.	huic	huic	huic	to (for) this
gen.	hújus	hújus	hújus	of this

Plural

	M	F	N	
nom.	hí	hae	haec	those
acc.	hós	hás	haec	those
abl.	hís	hís	hís	with (by) those
dat.	hís	hís	hís	to (for) those
gen.	hórum	hárum	hórum	of those

Demonstrative Adjectives and Pronouns

ille   illa   illud

Singular

	M	F	N	
nom.	**ille**	**illa**	**illud**	that
acc.	**illum**	**illam**	**illud**	that
abl.	**illó**	**illá**	**illó**	with (by) that
dat.	**illí**	**illí**	**illí**	to (for) that
gen.	**illíus**	**illíus**	**illíus**	of that

Plural

	M	F	N	
nom.	**illí**	**illae**	**illa**	those
acc.	**illós**	**illás**	**illa**	those
abl.	**illís**	**illís**	**illís**	with (by) those
dat.	**illís**	**illís**	**illís**	to (for) those
gen.	**illórum**	**illárum**	**illórum**	of those

iste, ista, istud (that) is declined like ille, illa, illud

Intensive Adjectives and Pronouns

for emphasis

ipse   ipsa   ipsum

Singular

M		F		N	
ipse	himself	**ipsa**	herself	**ipsum**	itself
ipsum	himself	**ipsam**	herself	**ipsum**	itself
ipsó	with (by) himself	**ipsá**	with (by) herself	**ipsó**	with (by) itself
ipsí	to (for) himself	**ipsí**	to (for) herself	**ipsí**	to (for) itself
ipsíus	of himself	**ipsíus**	of herself	**ipsíus**	of itself

Plural

	M	F	N	
nom.	**ipsí**	**ipsae**	**ipsa**	themselves
acc.	**ipsós**	**ipsas**	**ipsa**	themselves
abl.	**ipsís**	**ipsís**	**ipsís**	with (by) themselves
dat.	**ipsís**	**ipsís**	**ipsís**	to (for) themselves
gen.	**ipsórum**	**ipsárum**	**ipsórum**	of themselves

Relative Pronoun and Adjective

quí   quae   quod

Singular

quí	who	**quae**	which	**quod**	that
quem	whom	**quam**	which	**quod**	that
quó	with (by) whom	**quá**	with (by) which	**quó**	with (by) that
cui	to (for) whom	**cui**	to (for) which	**cui**	to (for) that
cújus	whose	**cújus**	of which	**cújus**	of that

Plural

quí	who	**quae**	which	**quae**	that
quós	whom	**quás**	which	**quae**	that
quibus	with (by) whom	**quibus**	with (by) which	**quibus**	with (by) that
quibus	to (for) whom	**quibus**	to (for) which	**quibus**	to (for) that
quórum	whose	**quárum**	of which	**quórum**	of that

Interrogative Pronouns

for questions

quis   quis   quid

Singular

quis	who	**quis**	who	**quid**	what
quem	whom	**quem**	whom	**quid**	what
quó	with (by) whom	**quá**	with (by) whom	**quó**	with (by) what
cui	to (for) whom	**cui**	to (for) whom	**cui**	to (for) what
cújus	whose	**cújus**	whose	**cújus**	of what

Plural

quí	who	**quae**	who	**quae**	what
quós	whom	**quás**	whom	**quae**	what
quibus	with (by) whom	**quibus**	with (by) whom	**quibus**	with (by) what
quibus	to (for) whom	**quibus**	to (for) whom	**quibus**	to (for) what
quórum	whose	**quárum**	whose	**quórum**	of what

Adjectives

describe nouns

Adjectives must agree with the noun they describe:

in gender (m, f, n)   **in number** (singular or plural)

in case (nom. acc. abl. dat. gen.) not declension (1,2,3,4,5).

Adjectives declensions are 1st, 2nd, 2nd neuter, 3rd and 3rd neuter.

2nd decl. (masculine) 1st decl. (feminine) 2nd decl. (neuter)

us   **a**   **um**

magn(**us**, **a**, **um**): large, great

3rd decl. (masculine) 3rd decl. (feminine) 3rd decl. (neuter)

is   **is**   **e**

difficil(**is**, **is**, **e**): difficult, hard

Colors Colores

color, coloris (m) color	3rd declension noun
albus, alba, album white	2m, 1f, 2n decl. adjective
caeruleus, **caerulea**, **caeruleum** blue	2, 1, 2n adj
canus, cana, canum gray	2, 1, 2n adj
coccineus, **coccinea**, **coccineum** scarlet	2, 1, 2n adj
flavus, flava, flavum yellow	2, 1, 2n adj
fulvus, fulva, fulvum brown	2, 1, 2n adj
niger, **nigra**, **nigrum** black	2, 1, 2n adj
purpureus, **purpurea**, **purpureum** purple	2, 1, 2n adj
rosaceus, **rosacea**, **rosaceum** pink, rose	2, 1, 2n adj
ruber, **rubra**, **rubrum** red	2, 1, 2n adj
violaceus, **violacea**, **violaceum** violet	2, 1, 2n adj
viridis, **viridis**, **viride** green	3rd mfn adj

Second Declension Adjectives

masculine

	Singular	Plural	
nominative	**us**	**í**	subject of the sentence
accusative	**um**	**ó**	direct object
ablative	**ó**	**ís**	object of preposition
dative	**ó**	**ís**	indirect object (to, for)
genitive	**í**	**órum**	possessive (of) ('s)

2nd declension adjectives that end in **er** (integer, a, um)
are declined like ager.

First Declension Adjectives

feminine

	Singular	Plural	
nominative	**a**	**ae**	subject of the sentence
accusative	**am**	**ás**	direct object
ablative	**á**	**ís**	object of preposition
dative	**ae**	**ís**	indirect object (to, for)
genitive	**ae**	**árum**	possessive (of) ('s)

Second Declension Neuter Adjectives

	Singular	Plural	
nominative	**um**	**a**	subject of the sentence
accusative	**um**	**a**	direct object
ablative	**ó**	**ís**	object of preposition
dative	**ó**	**ís**	indirect object (to, for)
genitive	**í**	**órum**	possessive (of) ('s)

Third Declension Adjectives
masculine and feminine

	Singular	Plural	
nominative	**is**	**és**	subject of the sentence
accusative	**em**	**és**	direct object
ablative	**í**	**ibus**	object of preposition
dative	**í**	**ibus**	indirect object (to, for)
genitive	**is**	**ium**	possessive (of) ('s)

Third Declension Neuter Adjectives

	Singular	Plural	
nominative	**e**	**ia**	subject of the sentence
accusative	**e**	**ia**	direct object
ablative	**í**	**ibus**	object of preposition
dative	**í**	**ibus**	indirect object (to, for)
genitive	**is**	**ium**	possessive (of) ('s)

Adjectives

*absconditus, a, um	hidden	2nd 1st 2nd n
acidus (m) a (f) um (n)	sour, tart	2nd 1st 2nd n
adultus, a, um	mature, adult	2nd 1st 2nd n
*aequus, a, um	equal, right	2nd 1st 2nd n
*aeternus, a, um	eternal	2nd 1st 2nd n
*in aeternum	forever	
aliqui, -qua, -quod	some	
*almus, a, um	kind, dear	2nd 1st 2nd n
*acer, acris, acre	sharp, stinging	3rd mfn
*altus, a, um	tall	2nd 1st 2nd n
amictus, a, um	clothed	2nd 1st 2nd n
*angelicus, a, um	angelic	2nd 1st 2nd n
anonymus, a, um	without a name	2nd 1st 2nd n
*antiquus, a, um	old	2nd 1st 2nd n
aquilonius, a, um	northernly	2nd 1st 2nd n
*ardens, ardentis	ardent, burning,	3rd mfn
austrinus, a, um	southernly	2nd 1st 2nd n
azymus, a, um	unleavened	2nd 1st 2nd n
*benignus, a, um	kind, loving	2nd 1st 2nd n
*bonus, a, um	good	2nd 1st 2nd n
*brevis, is, e	short, little	3rd mfn
*caecus, a, um	blind	2nd 1st 2nd n
*caldus, a, um	hot	2nd 1st 2nd n
captivus, a, um	caught, captured	2nd 1st 2nd n
carus, a, um	dear	2nd 1st 2nd n
*catholicus, a, um	universal, Catholic	2nd 1st 2nd n
ceterus, a, um	the other, rest of	2nd 1st 2nd n
*cotidianus, a, um	daily	2nd 1st 2nd n
crudus, a, um	raw	2nd 1st 2nd n
*cupidus, a, um	eager, desirous	2nd 1st 2nd n
*dexter, a, um	right	2nd 1st 2nd n

*difficilis, is, e	difficult, hard	3rd mfn
*dignus, a, um	worthy	2nd 1st 2nd n
dissimilis, is, e	unlike	3rd mfn
distinctus, a, um	distinct, separate	2nd 1st 2nd n
*dulcis, is, e	sweet	3rd mfn
*durus, a, um	hard, lasting	2nd 1st 2nd n
*facilis, is, e	easy	3rd mfn
*falsus, a, um	false	2nd 1st 2nd n
fatuus, a, um	foolish, silly	2nd 1st 2nd n
*felix, felicis	happy	3rd
ferreus, a, um	iron	2nd 1st 2nd n
festivus, a, um	pleasant, agreeable	2nd 1st 2nd n
*formosus, a, um	handsome	2nd 1st 2nd n
*fortis, is, e	strong	3rd mfn
*frigidus, a, um	cold	2nd 1st 2nd n
*gloriosus, a, um	famous, glorious	2nd 1st 2nd n
gracilis, is, e	graceful	3rd mfn
*gravis, is, e	serious	3rd mfn
hodiernus, a, um	today's	2nd 1st 2nd n
humidus, a, um	wet	2nd 1st 2nd n
*illicitus, a, um	unlawful	2nd 1st 2nd n
immedicablis, is, e	incurable	3rd mfn
*impossiblis, is, e	impossible	3rd mfn
incoctus, a, um	raw, uncooked	2nd 1st 2nd n
*infirmus, a, um	weak	2nd 1st 2nd n
*iratus, a, um	angry	2nd 1st 2nd n
incolumis, is, e	uninjured, safe	3rd mfn
incommutabilis, is, e	unchangeable	3rd mfn
lassus, a, um	tired, weary	2nd 1st 2nd n
*liber, libra, librum	free	2nd 1st 2nd n
*longinquus, a, um	distant, far off	2nd 1st 2nd n
*longus, a, um	long	2nd 1st 2nd n

lucidus, **a**, **um**	shiny	2ⁿᵈ 1ˢᵗ 2ⁿᵈ n
macer, **a**, **um**	thin, skinny	2ⁿᵈ 1ˢᵗ 2ⁿᵈ n
*__malus__, **a**, **um**	bad, evil	2ⁿᵈ 1ˢᵗ 2ⁿᵈ n
*__magnus__, **a**, **um**	large, great	2ⁿᵈ 1ˢᵗ 2ⁿᵈ n
*__mansuetus__, **a**, **um**	tame, meek, humble	2ⁿᵈ 1ˢᵗ 2ⁿᵈ n
maturus, **a**, **um**	ripe, mature	2ⁿᵈ 1ˢᵗ 2ⁿᵈ n
*__medius__, **a**, **um**	central, middle	2ⁿᵈ 1ˢᵗ 2ⁿᵈ n
meliusculus, **a**, **um**	a little better	2ⁿᵈ 1ˢᵗ 2ⁿᵈ n
*__mirabilis__, **is**, **e**	wonderful	3ʳᵈ mfn
*__miser__, **a**, **um**	unhappy, miserable	2ⁿᵈ 1ˢᵗ 2ⁿᵈ n
*__mitis__, **is**, **e**	mild, gentle	3ʳᵈ mfn
mollis, **is**, **e**	soft	3ʳᵈ mfn
*__multus__, **a**, **um**	much, (pl) many	2ⁿᵈ 1ˢᵗ 2ⁿᵈ n
navus, **a**, **um**	energetic, busy	2ⁿᵈ 1ˢᵗ 2ⁿᵈ n
*__noster__, **nostra**, **nostrum**	our	2ⁿᵈ 1ˢᵗ 2ⁿᵈ n
*__novus__, **a**, **um**	new	2ⁿᵈ 1ˢᵗ 2ⁿᵈ n
*__necessarius__, **a**, **um**	necessary	2ⁿᵈ 1ˢᵗ 2ⁿᵈ n
nonnullus, **a**, **um**	some, several	2ⁿᵈ 1ˢᵗ 2ⁿᵈ n
*__nullus__, **a**, **um**	no, not	2ⁿᵈ 1ˢᵗ 2ⁿᵈ n
*__obscurus__, **a**, **um**	dark	2ⁿᵈ 1ˢᵗ 2ⁿᵈ n
occidens, **occidentis**	setting, sunset, west	3ʳᵈ
*__occultus__, **a**, **um**	hidden, secret	2ⁿᵈ 1ˢᵗ 2ⁿᵈ n
*__oriens__, **-entis**	rising sun, morning, day, east	3ʳᵈ
*__parvulus__, **a**, **um**	small, tiny	2ⁿᵈ 1ˢᵗ 2ⁿᵈ n
*__paucus__, **a**, **um**	few	2ⁿᵈ 1ˢᵗ 2ⁿᵈ n
*__pauper__, **is**	poor, needy	3ʳᵈ
pedalis, **is**, **e**	foot long	3ʳᵈ mfn
pinguis, **is**, **e**	fat, juicy	3ʳᵈ mfn
*__pius__, **a**, **um**	pious, devout	2ⁿᵈ 1ˢᵗ 2ⁿᵈ n
ponderosus, **a**, **um**	heavy	2ⁿᵈ 1ˢᵗ 2ⁿᵈ n
potis or **pote**	able, possible	indeclinable
*__pretiosus__, **a**, **um**	precious	2ⁿᵈ 1ˢᵗ 2ⁿᵈ n pl

*profundus, a, um	deep	2nd 1st 2nd n pl
*pulcher, a, um	beautiful	2nd 1st 2nd n
quidam, quaedam, quoddam	certain	like qui, quae, quod
quietus, a, um	quiet	2nd 1st 2nd n
quisque, quaeque, quodque	each	
quot	how many	indeclinable
quotidanus, a, um	daily	2nd 1st 2nd n
rursus, a, um	backward, again	2nd 1st 2nd n
*sacer, sacra, sacrum	sacred	2nd 1st 2nd n
*sanctus, a, um	holy, blessed	2nd 1st 2nd n
*sapiens, sapientis	wise	3rd mfn
secretus, a, um	secret, separate	2nd 1st 2nd n
*similis, is, e	like, similar	3rd mfn
sincerus, a, um	real	2nd 1st 2nd n
*sinister, a, um	left	2nd 1st 2nd n
*stultus, a, um	foolish, stupid	2nd 1st 2nd n
*summus, a, um	highest, summit	2nd 1st 2nd n
*tantus, a, um	so great	2nd 1st 2nd n
tardus, a, um	slow	2nd 1st 2nd n
*tristis, is, e	sad	3rd mfn
tumultuosus, a, um	tumultuous, turbulent	2nd 1st 2nd n
*tutus, a, um	safe	2nd 1st 2nd n
ullus, a, um	any	2nd 1st 2nd n
*universus, a, um	all, universal	2nd 1st 2nd n
vacans, vacantis	vacant, empty	3rd mfn
*vacuus, a, um	empty	2nd 1st 2nd n
vehemens, vehementis	vehement, violent	3rd
*verus, a, um	true	2nd 1st 2nd n
vester, vestra, vestrum	your	2nd 1st 2nd n
voster, vostra, vostrum	your	2nd 1st 2nd n
*vivus, a, um	living	2nd 1st 2nd n

Comparative Adjectives

Adjectives are made comparative by removing the ending (**us**, **a**, **um**)
or (**is**, **is**, **e**) and replacing it with **ior** (m,f,n) or **ius** (n).

1st and 2nd declensions		3rd declension	
dignus, a, um	worthy	incolumis, is, e	safe
dignior (m,f)	more worthy	incolumior (m,f)	safer
dignius (n)	more worthy	incolumius (n)	safer

Superlative Adjectives

Adjectives are made superlative by removing the ending (**us**, **a**, **um**)
or (**is**, **is**, **i**) and replacing it with **issimus, a, um** (m,f,n).

dignissimus, a, um: most worthy

incolumissimus: safest

Exceptions

Adjectives ending in **lis**: add **limus, a, um**

gracilis, is, e (graceful): gracillus, a, um: most gracefully

Adjectives ending in **er**: add **rimus, a, um**.

acer, acra, acrum (sharp): acerrimus, a, um: sharpest

Irregular Adjectives

Positive	Comparative	Superlative
normal	more	most
parvulus, a, um small	**minor** (m, f) **minius** (n) smaller	**minimus, a, um** smallest
magnus, a, um large, great	**major** (m, f) **majus** (n) larger, greater	**maximus, a, um** largest, greatest
bonus, a, um good	**melior** (m, f) **melius** (n) better	**optimus, a, um** best
malus, a, um bad	**pejor, pejus** worse	**pessimus, a, um** worst
multus, a, um much	**plus** more	**plurimus, a, um** most
multi, ae, a many	**plus** more	**plurimi, ae, a** very many
novus, a, um new	**recentior** (m, f) **recentius** (n) more recent	**novissimus, a, um** last
vetus, a, um old	**vetiustior, vetustius** older	**veterrimus, a, um** oldest
juvenis, is, e young	**junior** (m, f) **junius** (n) younger, junior	**natu minimus, a, um** youngest
senex aged	**senior** (m, f) **senius** (n) elder, senior	**natu maximus, a, um** eldest
propinquus, a, um near	**proprior** (m, f) **proprius** (n) nearer	**proximus, a, um** nearest

Interjections
show emotion

ah	ah, ha, oh	**heu**	alas, oh	**hui**	hello, wow
aha	aha	**proh**	oh, ah		
ecce	behold	**vae**	woe to, alas		

Conjunctions

connect words

ac	and (before consonants)
adhuc	yet, now
antequam	before
aut	or
aut… aut	either… or
autem	however
at	but
atque	and
dum	while, until
dummodo	as long as
dumtaxet	insofar as
enim	for, yes, certainly
ergo	therefore
et	and
et… et	both… and
etsi	even if, although
etenim	for, as a matter of fact
immo	on the contrary, yes, no
namque	for, in fact
ne	and not, lest
nec	neither
necnon	also, besides
nec… nec	neither… nor
nisi	unless
non	not
nunc	now
prout	as, just as
quamvis	however, although
quia	because
-que	and
quod	because
sed	but
seu… seu	whether… or
si	if
seu… seu	whether… or
sive… sive	whether… or
non modo	not only…
sed etiam	but also
tametsi	even if, although
vero	but, truly

Everyday Expressions

Ita, **paululum linguae Latinae cognosco**!

Yes, I know a little Latin.

Salve!	Hello!
Salvete discipuli! (m) **ae** (f)	Hello students!
Salvete magister (magistra)!	Hello teacher!
Valete discipuli (ae)!	Good-bye students!
Vale magister (magistra)!	Good-bye teacher!
Die dulci fruere!	Have a nice day!
Dice (sing.) **dicite** (pl.) **in Latine.**	Say in Latin.
Latine reddere:	Translate into Latin.
Quid est nomen tuum?	What is your name?
Nomen meum est…	My name is…
Felix gentalis die.	Happy Birthday.
Quid tempus est?	What time is it?
Quomodo tu agens hodie?	How are you doing today?
Bene! Male.	Well. Poorly.
Obsecro!	Please!
Ita?	Really?
Etiam. Ita.	Yes.
Non.	No.
Si placet.	Please.
Gratias ago tibi.	Thank you.
Deus te (vos) pl. **benedicat.**	May God bless you.
Ave!	Greetings! Hail!
Quo vadis?	Where are you going?
Quid agens?	What are you doing?
Quid est?	What is it?
Quid nunc?	What now (next)?
Tuum est?	Is it yours?

Me paenitet.	I'm sorry.
Ne obliviscaris.	Don't forget.
Quantum scio.	As far as I know.
Ubi latrina est?	Where is the restroom?
Ubi gentium?	Where in the world?
Nolite perturbare.	Do not disturb.
Nolite intrare.	Keep out.
Tace! (sing) **Tacete**! (pl)	Quiet!
Cave canem!	Beware of dog!
Adsum.	I am present! Here!
Hoc mihi placet.	This pleases me.
Hoc non mihi placet.	This displeases me.
Tempus fugit.	Time flies.
In anno Domini. AD	In the year of Our Lord.
In se.	In itself.
Pro tempore.	For a time.
Non nunc.	Not now.
Eu! Euge!	Bravo. Well done!
Pro nunc.	For now.
Ningit.	It is snowing.
Postscriptum.	Postscript. PS
Volo ut mecum adsis.	Wish you were here.
Ite, lumen viride est.	Go, the light is green.
Flamma!	Fire!
Ait.	He (or she) said.
Hama pullí tostí.	A pail of fried chicken.
Da mihi crustum Etruscum cum caseó.	Give me a cheese pizza.

Adverbs

Adverbs tell how, where, why, etc. and often end in the letters **ly** in English. Adverbs are often made by subtracting **us**, **a**, **um** from an adjective and adding **e** or adding **iter** to the end of an adjective. Others are specific words.

rectus, a, um   recte (rightly)

This list gives irregularly formed adverbs:

abundanter	fully	**forsitan**	perhaps
adeo	precisely	**gradatim**	gradually
admodum	to the limit, yes	**haud**	not, hardly
aeque	fairly, equally	**heri**	yesterday
aliquid	somewhat	**hic**	here
aliquot	to some place	**hodie**	today
antea	formerly	**honeste**	honorably
aperte	openly	**humiliter**	humbly
autem	however	**ibi**	there
bene	well	**idcirco**	on that account
caute	carefully	**ideo**	therefore
ceu	as, if, just as	**igitur**	therefore
cito	quickly	**illic**	there, in that place
clam	secretly	**immediate**	immediately
cras	tomorrow	**immerito**	undeservedly
confestim	immediately	**immo**	on the contrary
continuo	immediately	**impie**	wickedly
cotidie	every day	**incessanter**	continually
dehinc	from now on, next	**inde**	from there
deinde	from that place, then	**inique**	unjustly
demum	precisely, exactly	**innocenter**	innocently
denique	finally, at last	**interea**	meanwhile
dum	while	**interius**	inwardly
durante	during	**inutiliter**	uselessly
enim	for	**item**	likewise
etenim	for	**inde**	from there, thereafter
etiam	also, yes	**interdum**	occasionally
etsi	even if	**iterum**	again
extrinsecus	outwardly	**invicem**	one another
fatue	foolishly	**ita**	so, thus
feliciter	happily	**itaque**	and so, therefore
fere	almost	**jam**	yet, right away
firmiter	strongly	**juxta**	nearby
foras	out, outside	**leniter**	gently

magnopere	greatly, very much	**quisque**	each
modo	only, just now	**quisquis**	whoever, whatever
necnon	also, moreover	**quo**	where
nempe	certainly, naturally	**quoad**	how far, how long
nimis	exceedingly	**quodammodo**	in a way
nuper	recently	**quolibet**	anywhere you please
nequaquam	no, by no means	**quomodo**	how
neque	not, neither… nor	**quoquo**	wherever
neve	and not	**quoties**	how many times
nondum	not yet	**quousque**	how far, how long
numquam	never	**retrorsum**	backwards, behind
nusquam	nowhere	**rursus**	on the contrary, back
olim	once upon a time	**scilicet**	of course, certainly
omnino	altogether	**secrete**	secretly, separately
paululum	a little	**semel**	once, at any time
praesertim	principally	**semper**	always
primó	at the beginning	**sic**	thus, also
prium	in the first place	**sicut**	as
prius	before, previously	**simul**	likewise, also
prope	near, nearby	**taliter**	to such a degree
propemodum	nearly, practically	**tam**	to such a degree
propterea	therefore	**tamen**	nevertheless, still
quam	how much	**tametsi**	even if, although
quamdiu	how long	**tamquam**	as, like
quamquam	although	**tandem**	finally, at last
quamque	especially	**tantopere**	so much
quam ob rem	why, for what reason	**tantum**	so greatly, so much
quam primum	as soon as possible	**tantummodo**	only
quamvis	although, however	**tarde**	slowly
quando	when	**tum**	then, next
quantum	to what extent	**tunc**	then, at that time
quapropter	wherefore, why	**ubi**	where
quare	why, wherefore	**ubicumque**	wherever
quatenus	how far	**ubique**	everywhere
quasi	like, nearly, almost	**unde**	whence
quasi modo	as in like manner	**usque**	all the way
quantopere	how much	**usquequo**	how long
quemadmodum	how, in what way	**utique**	anyhow
quid	what	**valde**	greatly, exceedingly
quidem	indeed, in fact	**vere**	truly
quidquid	whatever	**verumtamen**	nevertheless
quicumque	whoever, whatever	**vulgo**	commonly, generally
quippe	of course, indeed		

Comparative and Superlative Adverbs

Adverbs are made comparative by adding **ius** to the stem.

They are made superlative by adding **issimé** to the stem.

If an adverb ends in **iter**, those letters are removed before adding **ius** or **issimé**.

Exceptions

To make adverbs ending in **le** superlative: add **limé**.

facile (easily)   **facilius** (more easily)   **facillimé** (easily)

To make adverbs ending in **re** superlative: add **rimé**.

liberé (freely)   **liberius** (more freely)   **liberrimé** (most freely)

Irregular Adverbs

Positive	Comparative	Superlative
normal	more	most
bene	**melius**	**optimé**
well	better	best
magnopere, a, um	**magis**	**maximé**
greatly	more greatly	most greatly
male	**pejus**	**pessimé**
bad	worse	worst

Verbs

action words

Latin is a very concise language because the pronoun is often contained in the verb. Pronouns are used to describe "who" or "what." The list given below gives personal pronouns. Latin verbs follow this same pattern.

- 1st person: I   singular   **ego**   we   plural   **nos**
- 2nd person: you   singular   **tu**   you   plural   **vos**
- 3rd person: he, she, it   singular   **is, ea, id**   they plural   **ei, eae, ea**

There are four conjugations of verbs and the vocabulary list tells the conjugation of each verb: I, II, III, IV.

Second Principal Parts Endings
of the Four Conjugations

I   áre   II   ére   III   ere   IV   íre

Conjugating a Verb

The various tenses describe present, past or conditional action. The ending of a verb gives its meaning. Verb endings are added to the stem formed from one of its four principal parts. All four principal parts must be memorized in order to properly conjugate a verb in its tenses.

Moods of Verbs

Moods of verbs include: **indicative, subjunctive** and **imperative**.

Indicative mood is used for conversation and main clauses of sentences.

Subjunctive mood is used to express purpose and for conditional clauses.

Imperative mood is used for commands and addressing people by name.

Four Principal Parts (pp) of Verbs

The verb **audio** has four principal parts: **audio**, **audíre**, **audivi**, **auditus, a, um**

audio

First Principal Part: is the Present Tense, Active Voice, First Person Singular

It means: I hear.

The Present Stem (1st pp -o) audi forms:

Indicitive Mood	Subjunctive Mood
Present, Imperfect and Future Tenses	Present Tense
Active and Passive Voices	Active and Passive Voices

audíre

Second Principal Part: is the infinitive

It means: to hear

The Present Active Infinitive forms:

Subjunctive Mood
Imperfect Tense
Active and Passive Voices

audivi

Third Principal Part: is the Perfect Tense, Active Voice, First Person Singular

It means: I heard.

The Perfect Stem (3rd pp -i) audivi forms:

Indicitive Mood	Subjunctive Mood
Perfect, Pluperfect, Future Perfect Tenses	Perfect and Pluperfect Tense
(Active Voice)	(Active Voice)

auditus, a, um

Fourth Principal Part: is the Perfect Passive Participle

It means: Having been heard

The Perfect Passive Participle forms:

Indicitive Mood	Subjunctive Mood
perfect, pluperfect, future perfect tenses	perfect and pluperfect tense
(passive voice)	(passive voice)

Imperative Mood

I		II	
adjuvá	help!	**moné**	warn!
adjuváte	help! (pl)	**monéte**	warn! (pl)

III		IV	
mitte	send!	**audí**	listen!
mittite	send! (pl)	**audíte**	listen! (pl)

Accent Marks for Verbs

Although many accents marks are only used to make reading easier, always give accents for the 2nd Principal Part (**ére**), Imperative Plural (**éte**) and Imperfect Subjunctive forms of Second Conjugation verbs. This is needed to distinguish between Third Conjugation verbs. A long e (**érunt**) is used in Perfect Tense Indicitive Mood third person plural endings in all conjugations.

Verbs

IV	**abeo, abíre, abii, abitus, a, um**	go away
I	**abbrevio, abbreváre, abbrevavi, -atus**	shorten, cut off
III	**abduco, abducere, abduxi, abductus**	lead away
III	**abjicio, abjicere, abjeci, abjectus**	throw away, abandon
III	***abluo, abluere, ablui, ablutus**	cleanse, wash
I	**abrogo, abrogáre, abrogavi, abrogatus**	revoke, annul, abrogate
III	**abscedo, abscedere, -scessi, -cessus**	depart, retire
II	**abscido, abscidére, abscidi, abscisus**	cut off
III	***abscondo, abscondere, -di, -itus**	hide, conceal
III	***absolvo, absolvere, absolvi, -utus**	absolve, pardon
II	**absorbeo, absorbére, absorbui**	swallow, absorb
II	**abstergeo, abstergére, -si, -sus**	wipe away, blot out
II	**abstineo, abstinére, abstinui, -entus**	refrain, abstain
III	***accedo, accedere, accessi, accessus**	approach
III	**accendo, accendere, -di, -sus**	set on fire, enkindle
III	**accido, accidere, accidi**	occur, happen
III	***accipio, accipere, accepi, acceptus**	accept, receive

I	**accuso, accusáre, accusavi, accusatus**	accuse, blame
III	**acquiro, acquirere, acquisivi, acquisitus**	acquire, procure
III	**addico, addicere, addixi, addictus**	promise
III	***adduco, adducere, adduxi, adductus**	lead to, bring
IV	**adeo, adìre, adivi (ii), aditus**	come, approach
II	***adhaero, adhaerére, adhaesi, adhaesus**	stick to, adhere
II	**adhibeo, adhibére, adhibui, adhibitus**	invite, summon
II	***adimpleo, adimplére, -evi, adimpletus**	fill, fulfill
I	***adjuvo, adjuváre, adjuvi, adjuvatus**	help, assist
III	**admitto, admittere, admissi, admissus**	permit, grant
II	***admoneo, admonére, admonui, -itus**	admonish
I	***adoro, adoráre, adoravi, adoratus**	adore, worship
III	**adscribo, adscribere, -ipsi, -iptus**	ascribe, enroll
III	**adspicio, adspicere, -spexi, -spectus**	look at
irregular	***adsum, adesse, adfui, adfuturus**	be present
III	**adverto, advertere, adverti, advertus**	steer, direct
I	***aedifico, aedificáre, aedificavi, -atus**	built, construct
II	***aegreo, aegrére, aegrevi, aegretus**	be sick
I	***aestimo, aestimáre, aestimavi, -atus**	estimate, consider
III	**afficio, afficere, affeci, affectus**	affect, influence
III	***ago, agere, egi, actum**	do, drive
I	***ambulo, ambuláre, ambulavi, -atus**	walk
I	***amo, amáre, amavi, amatus**	love
IV	***aperio, aperíre, aperui, aperitus**	open
II	***appario, apparére, apparui, aparitus**	appear
I	***appello, appelláre, appellavi, -atus**	call, name
I	***appropinquo, -áre, -avi, -atus**	approach
II	**ardeo, ardére, arsi, arsus**	glow, burn
I	**armo, armáre, armavi, armatus**	arm, equip
III	**ascendo, ascendere, ascendi, -sus**	ascend, climb
III	***aspergo, aspergere, aspersi, -sum**	sprinkle, scatter
III	**vassisto, assistere, astiti**	assist, defend
II	****audeo, audére, ausus sum**	dare, venture

IV	*audio, audíre, audivi, auditus	hear
III	*benedico, -ere, benedixi, benedictus	bless, (praise w. dat.)
II	beneplaceo, -ére, -placui, -placitus	be pleasing to
III	*bibo, bibere, bibi, bibitus	drink
I	bino, bináre, binavi, binatus	duplicate
I	brevio, breviáre, breviavi, -iatus	shorten, condense
III	*cado, cadere, cecidi, casus	fall
III	caedo, -ere, cecidi, caesus	cut, kill
III	calefacio, calefacere, -feci, -tus	warm
I	*canto, cantáre, cantavi, cantatus	sing
III	*capio, capere, cepi, captus	seize, take
II	careo, carére, carui, caritus	lack
II	*caveo, cavére, cavi, cautus	beware, avoid
III	*cedo, cedere, cessi, cessus	yield, grant
I	*celebro, celebráre, -avi, -atus	celebrate
III	censeo, censere, censui, census	think
I	cito, citáre, citavi, citatus	excite, summon, call
I	*clamo, clamáre, clamavi, clamatus	shout, cry out
III	coepio, coepere, coepi, coeptum	began
I	*cogito, cogitáre, cogitavi, -atus	think
III	cogo, cogere, coegi, coactus	compel, gather
III	*cognosco, cognoscere, -novi, -nitus	know, be aquainted with
I	colligo, colligáre, colui, cultus	cultivate, bind
II	colo, colére, colui, cultus	celebrate, worship
I	combino, -áre, combinavi, -atus	combine, unite
III	comburo, -ere, combussi, combustus	to burn, consume
III	comedo, comedere, comedi, comesus	eat
I	*commemoro, -áre, -avi, -atus	commemorate
I	*commendo, -áre, commendavi, -atus	commend
II	commisceo, -ére, -miscui, -mixtus	mix, mingle
II	commoveo, -ére, -movi, -motus	excite, move
I	*communico, -áre, -avi, -atus	communicate

I	*comparo, comparáre, comparavi, -atus	prepare
II	*complaceo, complacére, -cui, -itus	please
III	comprehendo, -ere, -ensi, -ensus	to comprehend
II	*compleo, complére, complevi, -etus	fill up, complete
III	*compono, componere, composui, -itus	compose, arrange
I	computo, computáre, computavi, -atus	compute, count
I	condemno, condemnáre, -avi, -atus	condemn
III	condo, condere, condidi, conditus	found, create
III	confacio, conficere, confeci, confectus	finish
II	condoleo, condolére, condolui	have compassion
III	*confido, confidere, confessus sum	trust, confide in
I	configuro, configuráre, -avi, -atus	shape, form
II	***confiteor, confitéri, confessus	confess, praise
I	*confirmo, confirmáre, -avi, -atus	strengthen, confirm
I	*conforto, confortáre, confortavi, -atus	encourage, strengthen
III	confundo, confundere, -undi, -usus	confound, confuse
II	congaudeo, congaudére, congavisus	rejoice with
I	congrego, congregáre, congregavi, -atus	congregate
III	conjungo, conjungere, conjunxi, -junctus	join, unite
I	***conor, conári, conatus sum	attempt, try
III	conscribo, conscribere, -scripsi, -scriptus	enlist, compose
I	consecro, consecráre, -avi, consecratus	consecrate, sanctify
IV	*consentio, consentíre, -sensi, -sensum	consent, agree
I	*conservo, conserváre, conservavi, -atus	preserve, keep
I	considero, consideráre, consideravi, -atus	look, consider
I	consolido, consolidáre, consolidavi, -atus	strengthen
III	conspicio, conspicere, conspexi, -spectus	notice
III	constituo, constitere, constitui, -stitutus	appoint, constitute
III	construo, construere, construxi, -structus	build, construct
I	*consulto, consultáre, consultavi, -sultatus	ponder, consult
III	contemno, contemnere, -tempsi, -temptus	despise, show contempt
III	*contendo, contendere, contendi, contentus	fight, hasten

II	*contineo, continére, continui, -tentus	contain, enclose
III	*converto, convertere, -versi, -versus	change, convert
III	*convalesco, convalescere, convalui	recover
I	coopero, cooperáre, cooperavi, -atus	cooperate
I	coordino, coordináre, coordinavi, -atus	coordinate
III	coquo, coquere, -xi, -ctus	cook, bake, fry, roast
I	corono, coronáre, coronavi, coronatus	crown
III	*credo, credere, credidi, creditus	believe, trust in
I	*cremo, cremáre, cremavi, crematus	burn, cremate
I	*creo, creáre, creavi, creatus	create
III	*cupio, cupere, cupivi, cupitus	desire, long for
III	*curro, currere, cucurri, cursus	run
IV	*custodo, custodíre, custodivi, -itus	guard, watch
I	damno, damnáre, damnavi, -atus	condemn
II	*debeo, debére, debui, debitus	owe
I	dealbo, dealbáre, dealbavi, -atus	make white, cleanse
III	decerno, decernere, -revi, -retus	decide, discern
III	decido, decidere, decidi, decisus	fall down, perish
I	declino, declináre, declinavi, -atus	decline
I	decoro, decoráre, decoravi, -atus	adorn, decorate
III	dedo, dedere, dedidi, deditus	yield, surrender
III	deduco, deducere, deduxi, -uctus	lead down
III	*defendo, defendere, defendi, -sus	defend, protect
III	deficio, deficere, defeci, defectus	fail
I	degusto, -áre, -gustavi, -gustatus	taste, touch
I	delecto, delectáre, delectavi, -atus	delight, amuse
I	*demonstro, demonstráre, -avi, -atus	take down, put aside
III	depono, deponere, deposui, depositus	take down, put aside
III	deprimo, deprimere, depressi, depressus	depress, press down
III	descendo, descendere, -scendi, -scensus	descend
III	*describo, describere, descripsi, -scriptus	depict, describe
I	*desidero, desideráre, desideravi, -atus	desire, want
III	desisto, desistere, destiti, destitus	desist, give up

III	**despicio, despicere, despexi, -ectus**	despise
III	**destruo, destruere, destruxi, -uctus**	pull down, destroy
irr.	**desum, deese, defui, defuturus**	fail, be lacking
I	**devoro, devoráre, devoravi, -atus**	devour, waste
III	***dico, dicere, dixi, dictus**	speak
III	**differo, differe, distuli, dilatus**	spread, scatter
I	**dilato, dilitáre, dilitavi, dilitatus**	dilate, stretch
III	***diligo, diligere, dilexi, dilectus**	love, esteem
III	***dimitto, dimittere, dimisi, -issus**	dismiss
III	**discedo, discedere, discessi, -cessus**	separate, part
III	***dirigo, dirigere, direxi, directus**	direct, order
III	**discerno, discernere, decrevi, -cretus**	discern
III	***disco, discere, didici**	learn
III	**discedo, discedere, discessi, -cessus**	leave, depart
I	**dispenso, dispensáre, -avi, -atus**	dispense, distribute
III	**divido, dividere, dividi, divisus**	divide
I	***do, dáre, dedi, datus**	give
II	***doceo, docére, docui, doctus**	teach
II	**doleo, dolére, dolui, dolitus**	suffer
I	***dono, donáre, donavi, donatus**	give, donate
I	***dubito, dubitáre, dubitavi, -atus**	doubt
III	***duco, ducere, duxi, ductus**	lead
I	***duro, duráre, duravi, duratus**	harden, solidify
III	**edisco, ediscere, edidici**	memorize
III	**edoco, educere, edocui, edoctus**	deliver
III	**effundo, effudere, effudi, effusus**	pour out
III	***eligo, eligere, elegi, electus**	choose, select
I	**elevo, eleváre, elevavi, elevatus**	lift up, elevate
III	***emo, emere, emi, emptus**	buy
I	***enarro, enarráre, enarravi, -atus**	explain, narrate
I	**enuntio, enuntáre, enuntavi, -iatus**	announce, report
irr	***eo, íre, ivi or ii, itus**	go
III	**erubesco, erubescere, erubui**	blush, turn red

IV	*esurio, esuríre, esurivi, esuritus	be hungry
III	*evanesco, evanescere, evanui	vanish, disappear
III	evolvo, evolvere, evolvi, evolutus	develop, evolve
I	*exalto, exaltáre, exaltavi, exaltatus	exalt, glorify
IV	*exaudo, exaudíre, exaudivi, -itus	hear
I	excito, excitáre, excitavi, excitatus	just as, as if
I	excuso, excusáre, excusavi, -atus	excuse
II	*exerceo, exercére, exercui, -itus	train, exercise
I	*existimo, existimáre, -avi, -atus	think
I	*expecto, expectáre, -avi, -atus	wait, expect
III	*expello, expellere, expuli, expulsus	drive out, expel
I	expio, expiáre, expiavi, expiatus	cleanse, expiate
I	explico, explicáre, explicavi, -atus	unfold
III	***exsequor, exsequi, exsecutus sum	execute, perform
I	*exsulto, exsultáre, exsultavi, -atus	rejoice
I	exsuscito, exsuscitáre, -avi, -atus	awaken
III	*facio, facere, feci, factus	do, make, build
irr	*fero, ferre, tuli, latus	bear, carry
II	*frango, frangére, fregi, fractus	break, crush
III	***fruor, frui, fructus	enjoy
II	**gaudeo, gaudére, gavisus sum	rejoice, be glad
III	*gero, gerere, gessi, gestus	wear, wage (war)
I	*guberno, gubernáre, -avi, -atus	govern, pilot
II	*habeo, habére, habui, habitus	have, hold
I	*habito, habitáre, habitavi, -atus	dwell, abide
II	*haereo, haerére, haesi, haesus	stick, cling, hold
I	*honoro, honoráre, honoravi, -atus	honor
I	**hortor, hortárí, hortatus sum	exhort, encourage
I	*illumino, illumináre, -avi, -atus	illuminate
I	*immolo, immoláre, immolavi, -atus	sacrifice, immolate
I	*immuto, immutáre, immutavi, -atus	change
I	*impetro, impetráre, impetravi, -atus	obtain
II	impleo, implére, implevi, impletus	fill up, make full

I	**implico, implicáre, implicavi, -atus**	entangle
I	**imploro, implorále, imploravi, -atus**	implore
III	**impono, imponere, imposui, impositus**	put on, place on
III	**incido, incidere, incidi, incisus**	cut into
III	***incipio, incipere, incepi, inceptus**	begin
I	***interrogo, interrogáre, interrogavi, -atus**	ask
I	**inclino, inclináre, inclinavi, inclinatus**	bow, incline
II	***indulgeo, indulgére, indulsi, indultus**	forgive, grant
II	**inhaereo, inhaerére, inhaesi, inhaesus**	stick fast, adhere
IV	**innutrio, innutríre, innutrivi, innutritus**	nourish
III	**inscribo, inscribere, inscripsi, -iptus**	inscribe
III	**interficio, interficere, interfeci, -tus**	kill, slay
IV	***introeo, introíre, introivi, introitus**	enter
II	****intueor, intueri, intuitus sum**	look at, behold
IV	**invenio, inveníre, inveni, inventus**	find, discover
I	**investigo, investigáre, -gavi, -gatus**	track, investigate
III	****irascor, irasci, iratus sum**	be angry
II	**jubeo, jubére, jussi, jussus**	order, command
I	*****jacto, jactáre, jactavi, jactatus**	throw, throw overboard
I	***judico, judicáre, judicavi, judicatus**	judge, examine
III	***jungo, jungere, junxi, junctus**	join, unite, connect
I	**juro, juráre, juravi, juratus**	swear
I	***laboro, laboráre, laboravi, laboratus**	work
I	**lacero, laceráre, laceravi, laceratus**	tear, lacerate
I	***lamento, lamentáre, lamentavi, -atus**	weep, lament
II	**lateo, latére, latui**	lie hidden, lurk
I	***laudo, laudáre, laudavi, laudatus**	praise
I	***lavo, laváre, lavavi, lavatus**	wash, bathe
II	***lego, legére, legi, lectus**	read
I	**levo, leváre, levavi, levatus**	lift up, lighten, stand
I	**libero, liberáre, liberavi, liberatus**	free, liberate
III	****loquor, loqui, locutus sum**	say, speak about
III	***ludo, ludere, lusi, lusus**	play

I	*magnifico, magnificáre, -cavi, -atus	cherish
III	maledico, maledicere, -dixi, -dictus	slander, injure
I	*manduco, manducáre, -avi, -atus	eat
I	manifesto, manifestáre, -avi, -atus	make manifest
I	maturo, maturáre, maturavi, -atus	ripen, hasten,
II	***misereor, misereri, misertus	have mercy
I	mitigo, mitigáre, mitigavi, -atus	soothe, calm
III	*mitto, mittere, misi, missus	send
II	moneo, monére, monui, monitus	warn
III	***morior, mori, mortuus sum	die
I	*monstro, monstráre, -avi, -atus	show
II	*moveo, movére, movi, motus	move
I	*mundo, mundáre, mundavi, -atus	cleanse, purify
IV	munio, muníre, munivi, munitus	fortify, defend
I	*muto, mutáre, mutavi, mutatus	alter, change
I	*narro, narráre, narravi, narratus	speak, relate
III	***nascor, nasci, natus sum	born, originate
I	*nato, natáre, natavi, natatus	swim
I	*navigo, navigáre, navigavi, -atus	sail, navigate
I	navo, naváre, navavi, navatus	work energetically
irr	*nolo, nolle, nolui	wish not, be unwilling
I	*novo, nováre, novavi, novatus	make new
I	*nuntio, nuntiáre, nuntiavi, nuntiatus	announce
IV	*obedio, obedíre, obedivi, obeditus	obey
III	***obliviscor, oblivisci, oblitus sum	forget
I	*observo, observáre, -avi, observatus	watch
III	*obstupesco, obstupescere, -cui	be paralyzed, stupefied
II	*obtineo, obtinére, obtinui obtentus	obtain, prevail
III	*occido, occidere, occididi, occisus	cut down, kill, slay
I	*occupo, occupáre, -avi, occupatus	occupy
I	*oro, oráre, oravi, oratus	pray
III	*ostendo, ostendere, ostendi, ostentus	show
III	*parco, parcere, peperci, parsus	spare, preserve

I	*paro, paráre, paravi, paratus	prepare, arrange
III	*pasco, pascere, pavi, pastus	feed
III	***patior, pati, passus sum	suffer, endure
III	*pello, pellere, pepuli, pulsus	drive, rout
III	*perdo, perdere, perdidi, perditus	crush, destroy
IV	*pereo, períre, perii, peritus	perish
II	pendeo, pendére, pependi	hang, depend
III	*pendo, pendere, pependi, pensus	weigh, pay
II	perfrigo, perfrigére, -fregi, -fractus	break into pieces
I	permuto, permutáre, permutavi, -atus	change thoroughly
II	*pertineo, pertinére, pertinui	pertain to
I	perturbo, perturbáre, -avi, -atus	disturb, bother
IV	*pervenio, perveníre, perveni, -ventus	arrive
III	*peto, petere, petivi, petitus	seek, ask
II	*placeo, placére, placui, placitus	please, satisfy
I	*planto, plantáre, plantavi, plantatus	plant, set
II	***polliceor, pollicéri, pollicitus sum	promise
III	*pono, ponere, posui, positus	put, place
I	*porto, portáre, portavi, portatus	carry
II	*possideo, possidére, possedi, -esus	possess, have
irr	*possum, posse, potui	be able, can
III	praescribo, -ere, -scripsi, -iptus	prescribe
II	*praevaleo, praevalére, praevalui	prevail
II	prohibeo, prohibére, prohibui, -itus	prohibit, prevent
III	***proficiscor, -isci, profectus sum	set out, begin
I	pugno, pugnáre, pugnavi, pugnatus	fight
I	pulso, pulsáre, pulsavi, pulsatus	strike against, batter
I	*purgo, purgáre, purgavi, purgatus	purge, cleanse
I	*puto, putáre, putavi, putatus	think
III	*quaero, quaerere, -sivi, -situs	search for, to acquire
III	rapio, rapere, rapui, raptus	seize, snatch
IV	*redeo, redìre, redivi (ii), reditus	return, give back
I	reformo, reformáre, reformavi, -atus	reshape, remake

I	*religo, religáre, religavi, religatus	fasten, bind
III	*relinquo, relinqere, relinqui, relictus	leave, abandon
II	*removeo, removére, removi, remotus	withdraw, remove
I	*renovo, nováre, renovavi, renovatus	make new, restore
III	*renuo, renuere, renui	reject, refuse
I	*reparo, reparáre, reparavi, reparatus	repair, restore
III	repello, repellere, repuli, repulsus	repell, drive back
III	*rependo, rependere, rependi, -sus	repay, return
III	*repeto, repetere, repetivi, (repetii), -itus	repeat
III	*requiesco, requiescere, -evi, -etus	be at rest
III	*requiro, requirere, requisivi, -itus	require, need
III	*resisto, resistere, restiti	resist, stop
II	*respondo, respondére, responsi, -sus	answer, reply
II	resplendeo, resplendére, resplendui	shine, show forth
II	*resurgo, resurgére, -exi, resurrectus	rise, rise from the dead
I	*revelo, reveláre, revelavi, revelatus	reveal, uncover
I	resuscito, resuscitáre, -avi, -atus	raise up, resuscitate
III	*retribuo, retribuere, retribui, -utus	repay, reward
III	revivo, revivere, revixi, revictus	revive
I	revoco, revocáre, revocavi, revocatus	recall
III	*revolvo, revolvere, revolvi, revolutum	unroll, revolve, smile
II	*rideo, ridére, risi, risus	laugh, smile
II	*rigo, rigáre, rigavi, rigatus	wash, moisten
I	*salvo, salváre, salvavi, salvatus	save
I	sanctifico, sanctificáre, -avi, -atus	sanctify
IV	*scio, scíre, scivi, scitus	know, understand
III	*scindo, scindere, scindi, scissus	cut, split
III	*scribo, scribere, scripsi, scriptus	write
II	*sedeo, sedére, sedi, sessus	sit
IV	*sentio, sentíre, sensi, sensus	perceive, sense
I	*separo, separáre, separavi, -atus	separate
I	*servo, serváre, servavi, servatus	protect
IV	*servo, servíre, servivi, servitus	serve

III	***sequor, sequi, secutus sum**	follow
IV	***sitio, sitíre, sitivi** or **sitii**	thirst
III	**solvo, solvere, solvi, solutus**	loosen, set sail
I	***specto, spectáre, spectavi, -atus**	view, look at
I	***spero, speráre, speravi, speratus**	hope for, expect
I	***spiro, spiráre, spiravi, spiratus**	breathe, exhale
II	***studeo, studére, studui**	desire, be eager for
irr	***sum, esse, fui, futurus**	be
I	**supplico, supplicáre, -avi, -atus**	supplicate
II	***surgo, surgére, surrexi, surrectus**	awake, rise
II	***sustineo, sustinére, sustinui, -tentus**	to sustain, endure
II	***taceo, tacére, tacui, tacitus**	be silent, quiet
III	***tango, tangere, tetigi, tactus**	touch
I	***tardo, tardáre, tardavi, tardatus**	delay
II	***teneo, tenére, tenui, tentus**	hold, keep
I	**turbo, turbáre, turbavi, turbatus**	disturb
III	***tollo, tollere, sustuli, sublatus**	lift, take
III	***vado, vadere, vasi**	go, walk
II	**valeo, valére, valui, valiturus**	be well, be strong
III	***vendo, vendere, vendidi**	sell, vend
IV	***venio, veníre, veni, ventus**	come
III	****verro, verrere, versus**	brush, sweep
III	***verto, vertere, verti, versus**	turn
II	***video, vidére, vidi, visus**	see
I	***vigilo, vigiláre, vigilavi, vigilatus**	watch
I	**visito, visitáre, visitavi, visitatus**	visit, survey
I	***vivifico, vivificáre, vivificavi, -atus**	bring to life
I	***voco, vocáre, vocavi, vocatus**	call
I	***volo, voláre, volavi, volatus**	fly
irr	**volo, vellere, volui**	wish, want
III	***volvo, volvere, volvi, volutus**	roll, turn around

**semi deponent—perfect tense uses passive forms with active meanings.

***deponent—looks passive but are translated active.

Verb Charts

Indicative Mood

Present Tense

Active Voice

1st pp -o + vowel of the conjugation (a, e, i) + o, s, t, mus, tis, nt

Third conjugation is irregular.

Translation

I help.	We help.
You help.	You (pl) help.
He, she, it, helps.	They help.

I		**II**	
adjuv**ó**	adjuv**ámus**	mon**eó**	mon**émus**
adjuv**ás**	adjuv**átis**	mon**és**	mon**étis**
adjuv**at**	adjuv**ant**	mon**et**	mon**ent**

III		**III** (io verbs)		**IV**	
duc**ó**	duc**imus**	cap**ió**	cap**imus**	aud**ió**	aud**ímus**
duc**is**	duc**itis**	cap**is**	cap**itis**	aud**ís**	aud**ítis**
duc**it**	duc**unt**	cap**it**	cap**iunt**	aud**it**	aud**iunt**

Present Tense

Passive Voice

1st pp -o + vowel of the conjugation a, e, i + or, ris, tur, mur, mini, ntur

Third conjugation is irregular.

Translation

I am being helped.	We are being helped.
You are being helped.	You (pl) are being helped.
He, she, it, is being helped.	They are being helped.

I		**II**	
adjuv**or**	adjuv**ámur**	mon**eor**	mon**émur**
adjuv**áris**	adjuv**ámini**	mon**éris**	mon**émini**
adjuv**átur**	adjuv**antur**	mon**étur**	mon**entur**

III		**III** (io verbs)		**IV**	
duc**or**	duc**imur**	cap**ior**	cap**imur**	aud**ior**	aud**ímur**
duc**eris**	duc**imini**	cap**eris**	cap**ímini**	aud**íris**	aud**ímini**
duc**itur**	duc**untur**	cap**itur**	cap**iuntur**	aud**itur**	aud**iuntur**

Imperfect Tense

Active Voice

1st pp -o + vowel of the conjugation a, e, e, ie + ba + m, s, t, mus, tis, nt

Translation

I was helping.	We were helping.
You were helping.	You (pl) were helping.
He, she, it, was helping.	They were helping.

I

adjuvábam	adjuvábámus
adjuvábás	adjuvábátis
adjuvábat	adjuvábant

II

monébam	monébamus
monébas	monébatis
monébat	monébant

III

ducébam	ducébámus
ducébás	ducébátis
ducébat	ducébant

III (io verbs)

capiébam	capiébámus
capiébás	capiébátis
capiébat	capiébant

IV

audiébam	audiébámus
audiébás	audiébátis
audiébat	audiébant

Imperfect Tense

Passive Voice

Translation

I was being helped.	We were being helped.
You were being helped.	You (pl) were being helped.
He, she, it, were being helped.	They were being helped.

1st pp -o + vowel of the conjugation a, e, e, ie + ba + r, ris, tur, mur, mini, ntur

I

adjuvábar	adjuvábámur
adjuvábáris	adjuvábámini
adjuvábátur	adjuvábantur

II

monébar	monébámur
monébáris	monébámini
monébátur	monébantur

III

ducébar	ducébámur
ducébáris	ducébámini
ducébátur	ducébantur

III (io verbs)

capiébar	capiébámur
capiébáris	capiébámini
capiébátur	capiébantur

IV

audiébar	audiébámur
audiébáris	audiébámini
audiébátur	audiébantur

Future Tense

Active Voice

I & II Conjugation

1st pp -o + vowel of the conjugation I a, II e, + bo + bi or bu + s, t, mus, tis, nt

Translation

I will (shall) help.	We will help.
You will help.	You (pl) will help.
He, she, it, will help.	They will help.

I		**II**	
adjuvábó	adjuvábimus	monébó	monébimus
adjuvábis	adjuvábitis	monébis	monébitis
adjuvábit	adjuvábunt	monébit	monébunt

III Conjugation	IV Conjugation
1pp -o + am, es, et, emus, etis, ent	1pp -o + iam, ies, iet, iemus, ietis, ient

III		**III** (io verbs)		**IV**	
ducam	ducémus	capiam	capiémus	audiam	audiémus
ducés	ducétis	capiés	capiétis	audiés	audiétis
ducet	ducent	capiet	capient	audiet	audient

Future Tense

Passive Voice

I & II Conjugation: 1st pp -o + vowel of the conjugation I a, II e

+ bor, beris, bitur, bimur, bimini, buntur

Translation

I shall be helped.	We will be helped.
You will be helped.	You (pl) will be helped.
He, she, it, will be helped.	They will be helped.

I		**II**	
adjuvábor	adjuvábimur	monébor	monébimur
adjuváberis	adjuvábiminí	monéberis	monébiminí
adjuvábitur	adjuvábuntur	monébitur	monébuntur

III Conjugation	1pp -o + ar, eris, etur, emur, emini, entur
IV Conjugation	1pp -o + iar, ieris, ietur, iemur, iemini, ientur

III		**III** (io verbs)		**IV**	
ducar	ducémur	capiar	capiémur	audiar	audiémur
ducéris	ducémini	capiéris	capiémini	audiéris	audiémini
ducétur	ducentur	capiétur	capientur	audiétur	audientur

Perfect Tense

Active Voice

3 pp+ i, isti, it, imus, istis, erunt

Translation

I helped.	We helped.
You helped.	You (pl) helped.
He, she, it, helped.	They helped.

I

adjuví	adjuvimus
adjuvistí	adjuvistis
adjuvit	adjuvérunt

II

monuí	monuimus
monuistí	monuistis
monuit	monuérunt

III and **III** io

duxí	duximus
duxistí	duxistis
duxit	duxérunt

IV

audiví	audivimus
audivistí	audivistis
audivit	audivérunt

Perfect Tense

Passive Voice

4 pp and sum, es, est, sumus, estis, sunt

Translation

I was being helped.	We were being helped.
You were being helped.	You (pl) were being helped.
He, she, it, was being helped.	They were being helped.

I

adjuvátus, a, um sum	adjuvátí, ae, a sumus
adjuvátus, a, um es	adjuvátí, ae, a estis
adjuvátus, a, um est	adjuvátí, ae, a sunt

II

monitus, a, um sum	monití, ae, a sumus
monitus, a, um es	monití, ae, a estis
monitus, a, um est	monití, ae, a sunt

III and **III** io

ductus, a, um sum	ductí, ae, a sumus
ductus, a, um es	ductí, ae, a estis
ductus, a, um est	ductí, ae, a sunt

IV

audítus, a, um sum	audítí, ae, a sumus
audítus, a, um es	audítí, ae, a estis
audítus, a, um est	audítí, ae, a sunt

Pluperfect Tense

Active Voice

3 pp –i + eram, eras, erat, eramus, eratis, erant

Translation

I had helped.	We had helped.
You had helped.	You (pl) had helped.
He, she, it, had helped.	They had helped.

I		II	
adjuv**eram**	adjuv**erámus**	monu**eram**	monu**erámus**
adjuv**erás**	adjuv**erátis**	monu**erás**	monu**erátis**
adjuv**erat**	adjuv**erant**	monu**erat**	monu**erant**

III and III io		IV	
dux**eram**	dux**erámus**	audiv**eram**	audiv**eramus**
dux**erás**	dux**erátis**	audiv**erás**	audiv**erátis**
dux**erat**	dux**erant**	audiv**erat**	audiv**erant**

Pluperfect Tense

Passive Voice

4 pp and eram, eras, erat, eramus, eratis, erant

Translation

I had been helped.	We had been helped.
You had been helped.	You (pl) had been helped.
He, she, it, had been helped.	They had been helped.

I		II	
adjuvátus, a, um eram	adjuvátí, ae, a eramus	monitus, a, um eram	monití, ae, a eramus
adjuvátus, a, um eras	adjuvátí, ae, a eratis	monitus, a, um eras	monití, ae, a eratis
adjuvátus, a, um erat	adjuvátí, ae, a erant	monitus, a, um erat	monití, ae, a erant

III and III io		IV	
ductus, a, um eram	ductí, ae, a eramus	audítus, a, um eram	audítí, ae, a eramus
ductus, a, um eras	ductí, ae, a eratis	audítus, a, um eras	audítí, ae, a eratis
ductus, a, um erat	ductí, ae, a erant	audítus, a, um erat	audítí, ae, a erant

Future Perfect Tense

Active Voice

3 pp+ ero, eris, erit, erimus, eritis, erunt

Translation

I will have helped.	We will have helped.
You will have helped.	You (pl) will have helped.
He, she, it,will have helped.	They will have helped.

I

adjuveró	adjuverimus
adjuveris	adjuveritis
adjuverit	adjuverunt

II

monueró	monuerimus
monueris	monueritis
monuerit	monuerunt

III and **III** io

duxeró	duxerimus
duxeris	duxeritis
duxerit	duxerunt

IV

audiveró	audiverimus
audiveris	audiveritis
audiverit	audiverunt

Future Perfect Tense

Passive Voice

4 pp and ero, eris, erit, erimus, eritis, erunt

Translation

I will have been helped.	We will have been helped.
You will have been helped.	You (pl) will have been helped.
He, she, it, will have been helped.	They will have been helped.

I

adjuvátus, a,um eró	adjuvátí, ae, a erimus
adjuvátus, a,um eris	adjuvátí, ae, a eritis
adjuvátus, a,um erit	adjuvátí, ae, a erunt

II

monitus, a,um eró	monití, ae, a erimus
monitus, a,um eris	monit, ae, a eritis
monitus, a,um erat	monit, ae, a erunt

III and **III** io

ductus, a,um eró	ductí, ae, a erimus
ductus, a,um eris	ductí, ae, a eritis
ductus, a,um erit	ductí, ae, a erunt

IV

audítus, a,um eró	audítí, ae, a erimus
audítus, a,um eris	audítí, ae, a eritis
audítus, a,um erit	audítí, ae, a erunt

Subjunctive Mood of Verbs

The subjunctive mood is used:

1) To express: **hope (may), wish (let us)** or a **command** in the first or third person. Negative commands are introduced by the word *ne*.

2) It is used in **subordinate clauses** introduced by the words *ut, uti, qui*, or *ne* to express purpose.

3) **Indirect question** (*si*) if.

4) **Cum clause** when *cum* means *since* or *when*.

5) **Ablative absolute** e.g. *dimittis peccatis tuis:* sins having been forgiven.

If the main verb is in the **primary tenses** present, future or future perfect indicative the verb in the subjunctive clause **uses the present or imperfect subjunctive**.

If the main verb is in the **secondary tenses** perfect, imperfect, or pluperfect indicative the verb in the subjunctive clause **uses the perfect or pluperfect subjunctive**.

Subjunctive Mood

Present Tense

Active Voice

1pp + I e II ea III a IV ia + active endings m, s, t, mus, tis, nt

Translation

That I may help.	That we may help.
That you may help.	That you (pl) may help.
That (he, she, it) may help.	That they may help.

I		**II**	
adjuv**em**	adjuv**émus**	mon**eam**	mon**eámus**
adjuv**és**	adjuv**étis**	mon**eás**	mon**eátis**
adjuv**et**	adjuv**ent**	mon**eat**	mon**eant**

III		**III** (io verbs)		**IV**	
duc**am**	duc**ámus**	cap**iam**	cap**imus**	aud**iam**	aud**iámus**
duc**ás**	duc**átis**	cap**iás**	cap**itis**	aud**iás**	aud**iátis**
duc**at**	duc**ant**	cap**iat**	cap**iunt**	aud**iat**	aud**iant**

Present Tense

Passive Voice

1pp + I e II ea III a IV ia + passive endings r, ris, tur, mur, mini, ntur
3rd conjugation is irregular

Translation

That I may be helped.	That we may be helped.
That you may be helped.	That you (pl) may be helped.
That (he, she, it,) may be helped.	That they may be helped.

I		**II**	
adjuv**er**	adjuv**émur**	mon**ear**	mon**eámur**
adjuv**éris**	adjuv**émini**	mon**eáris**	mon**eámini**
adjuv**étur**	adjuv**entur**	mon**eátur**	mon**eantur**

III		**III** (io verbs)		**IV**	
duc**ar**	duc**ámur**	cap**iar**	cap**iámur**	aud**iar**	aud**iámur**
duc**áris**	duc**ámini**	cap**iáris**	cap**iámini**	aud**iáris**	aud**iámini**
duc**átur**	duc**antur**	cap**iátur**	cap**iantur**	aud**iátur**	aud**iantur**

Imperfect Tense

Active Voice

2pp + active endings

Translation

That I might help.

That you might help.

That (he, she, it,) might help.

That we might help.

That you (pl) might help.

That they might help.

I

		II	
adjuvárem	adjuvárémus	monérem	monérémus
adjuvárés	adjuváretis	monérés	monérétis
adjuváret	adjuvárent	monéret	monérent

III and **III** io   **IV**

ducerem	ducerémus	audírem	audírémus
ducerés	ducerétis	audíres	audírétis
duceret	ducerent	audíret	audírent

Imperfect Tense

Passive Voice

2pp + passive endings

Translation

That I might be helped.

That you might be helped.

That (he, she, it,) might be helped.

That we might be helped.

That you (pl) might be helped.

That they might be helped.

I

		II	
adjuvárer	adjuváremur	monérer	monérémur
adjuváréris	adjuváreminí	monéréris	monérémíní
adjuváretur	adjuvárentur	monérétur	monérentur

III and **III** io   **IV**

ducerer	ducerémur	audírer	audírémur
duceréris	duceréminí	audíréris	audíréminí
ducerétur	ducerentur	audírétur	audírentur

Perfect Tense

Active Voice

3 pp+ erim, eris, erit, erimus, eristis, erint

Translation

(Whether) I helped.	(Whether) we helped.
(Whether) you helped.	(Whether) you (pl) helped.
(Whether) he, she, it, helped.	(Whether) they helped.

I

adjuv**erim**	adjuv**erímus**
adjuv**erís**	adjuv**erítis**
adjuv**erit**	adjuv**erint**

II

monu**erim**	monu**erímus**
monu**erís**	monu**erítis**
monu**erit**	monu**erint**

III and **III** io

dux**erim**	dux**erímus**
dux**erís**	dux**erítis**
dux**erit**	dux**erint**

IV

audiv**erim**	audiv**erímus**
audiv**erís**	audiv**erítis**
audiv**erit**	audiv**erint**

Perfect Tense

Passive Voice

4 pp and sim, sis, sit, simus, sitis, sint

Translation

(Whether) I was helped.	(Whether) we were helped.
(Whether) you were helped.	(Whether) you (pl) were helped.
(Whether) he, she, it, was helped.	(Whether) they were helped.

I

adjuvátus,a,um sim	adjuvátí,ae,a simus
adjuvátus,a,um sis	adjuvátí,ae,a sitis
adjuvátus,a,um sit	laudatí,ae,a sint

II

monitus sim	monití,ae,a simus
monitus sis	monití,ae,a sitis
monitus sit	monití,ae,a sint

III and **III** io

ductus,a,um sim	ductí,ae,a simus
ductus,a,um sis	ductí,ae,a sitis
ductus,a,um sit	ductí,ae,a sint

IV

auditus,a,um sim	audití,ae,a simus
auditus,a,um sis	audití,ae,a sitis
auditus,a,um sit	audití,ae,a sint

Pluperfect Tense

Active Voice

3 pp+ issem, isses, issit, issemus, issetis, issent

Translation

(Whether) I had helped.	(Whether) we had helped.
(Whether) you had helped.	(Whether) you (pl) had helped.
(Whether) he, she, it, had helped.	(Whether) they had helped.

I		**II**	
adjuv**issem**	adjuv**issémus**	monu**issem**	monu**issémus**
adjuv**issés**	adjuv**issétis**	monu**issés**	monu**issétis**
adjuv**isset**	adjuv**issent**	monu**isset**	monu**issent**

III and **III** io		**IV**	
dux**issem**	dux**issémus**	audiv**issem**	audiv**issémus**
dux**issés**	dux**issétis**	audiv**issés**	audiv**issétis**
dux**isset**	dux**issent**	audiv**isset**	audiv**issent**

Pluperfect Tense

Passive Voice

4 pp and sim, sis, sit, simus, sitis, sint

Translation

(Whether) I had been helped.	(Whether) we had been helped.
(Whether) you had been helped.	(Whether) you (pl) had been helped.
(Whether) he, she, it, had been helped.	(Whether) they had been helped.

I		**II**	
adjuvátus, a, um essem	laudatí, ae, a essemus	monitus, a, um essem	monití, ae, a essemus
adjuvátus, a, um esses	laudatí, ae, a essetis	monitus, a, um esses	monití, ae, a essetis
adjuvátus, a, um esset	laudatí, ae, a essent	monitus, a, um esset	monití, ae, a essent

III and **III** io		**IV**	
ductus, a, um essem	ductí, ae, a essemus	auditus, a, um essem	audití, ae, a essemus
ductus, a, um esses	ductí, ae, a essetis	auditus, a, um essetis	audití, ae, a essetis
ductus, a, um esset	ductí, ae, a essent	auditus, a, um essent	audití, ae, a essent

Infinitives

Present

		I			II	
Active	2pp	**adjuváre**	to help	**monére**	to warn	
Passive		**adjuvári**	to be helped	**monéri**	to be warned	

		III			IV	
Active	2pp	**mittere**	to send	**audíre**	to hear	
Passive		**mittí**	to be sent	**audíri**	to be heard	

Perfect

I-IV

Active	3pp + isse	**adjuvisse**	**monuisse**	to have helped	to have warned
		misisse	**audisse**	to have sent	to have heard

		I		II
Passive	4pp and esse	**adjuvatus, a, um esse**		**monitus, a, um esse**
		to have been helped		to have been warned

	III		IV
	missus, a, um esse		**auditus, a, um esse**
	to have sent		to have heard

Future

I-IV

Active	4pp —us + úrus and esse

	I	II
Active	**adjuvatúrus esse**	**monitúrus esse**
	to be about to help	to be about to warn

	III	IV
Active	**missúrus esse**	**auditúrus esse**
	to be about to send	to be about to hear

Passive	4pp (neuter form) and írí

	I	II
Passive	**adjuvátum írí**	**monitum írí**
	to be about to be helped	to be about to be warned

	III	IV
Passive	**missum írí**	**auditum írí**
	to be about to be sent	to be about to be heard

Participles

Present Active

Declined like nouns

1pp –o + the vowel of conjugation a, e, e, ie + ns or nt +3ʳᵈ decl. endings

translation: verb + ing

	I	**II**	**III**	**III** io	**IV**	
nom.	adjuvans	monens	mittens	capiens	audiens	**hearing**
acc.	adjuvantem	monentem	mittentem	capientem	audientem	**hearing**
abl.	adjuvante (í)	monente (í)	mittente (í)	capiente (í)	audiente (í)	**from hearing**
dat.	adjuvantí	monentí	mittentí	capientí	audientí	**to (for) hearing**
gen.	adjuvantis	monentis	mittentis	capientis	audientis	**of hearing**

Ablative: (e) when used verbally with an object

(í) when used as an attributal adjective

Perfect

I-IV

Passive   4 pp   declined with m/f/n us, a, um endings   having been…

Future

I-IV

Active   4pp –us, a, um +urus   about to warn

Gerunds and Gerundives

A gerund is an active voice verbal noun that is singular in tense. It is like a gerundive, but is only used in the acc. abl. dat. and gen. cases neuter.

Gerundives are passive verbal adjectives, translated with an -ing added to the word, that are created by adding **nd** + **us**, **a**, **um** endings to a verb.

Irregular Verbs

Indicitive Mood

Present Tense

to be	be able	wish	not wish	go
sum	possum	volo	nolo	eo
es	potes	vis	non vis	is
est	potest	vult	non vult	it
sumus	póssumus	vólumus	nólumus	imus
estis	potéstis	vultis	non vultis	itis
sunt	possunt	volunt	nolunt	eunt

Imperfect Tense (was …ing)

eram	póteram	volébam	nolébam	ibam
erás	póteras	volébás	nolébás	ibás
erat	póterat	volébat	nolébat	ibat
erámus	poterámus	volébámus	nolébámus	ibámus
erátis	poterátis	volébátis	nolébátis	ibátis
errant	póterant	volébant	nolébant	ibant

Future Tense (will or shall)

eró	pótero	volam	nolam	ibo
eris	póteris	volés	nolés	ibis
erit	póterit	volet	nolet	ibit
erimus	potérimus	volémus	nolémus	ibimus
eritis	potéritis	volétis	nolétis	ibitis
erunt	póterunt	volent	nolent	ibunt

Indicitive Mood

Perfect Tense (-ed)

fuí	pótui	volui	nolui	ii
fuísti	potuísti	voluisti	noluisti	isti
fuit	pótuit	voluit	noluit	it
fúimus	potúimus	voluimus	noluimus	iimus
fuístis	potuístis	voluístis	noluístis	istis
fuérunt	potuérunt	voluérunt	noluérunt	iérunt

Pluperfect Tense (had)

fueram	potúeram	volúeram	nolúeram	ieram
fúeras	potúeras	volúeras	nolúeras	ieras
fúerat	potúerat	volúerat	nolúerat	ierat
fuerámus	potuerámus	voluerámus	noluerámus	ieramus
fuerátis	potuerátis	voluerátis	noluerátis	ieratis
fúerant	potúerant	volúerant	nolúerant	ierant

Future Perfect Tense (will have)

fúero	potúero	volúero	nolúero	iero
fúeris	potúeris	volúeris	nolúeris	ieris
fúerit	potúerit	volúerit	nolúerit	ierit
fuérimus	potuérimus	voluérimus	noluérimus	ierimus
fuéritis	potuéritis	voluéritis	noluéritis	ieritistis
fúerunt	potuerunt	voluerunt	nolerunt	ierunt

Subjunctive Mood

Present Tense (may)

sim	possim	velim	nolim	eam
sís	possís	velís	nolís	eas
sit	possit	velit	nolit	eat
símus	possímus	velímus	nolímus	eamus
sítis	possítis	velítis	nolítis	eatis
sint	possint	velint	nolint	eant

Imperfect Tense (might)

essem	possem	vellem	nollem	irem
esses	posses	velles	nolles	ires
esset	posset	vellet	nollet	iret
essémus	possémus	vellémus	nollémus	irémus
essétis	possétis	vellétis	nollétis	irétis
essent	possent	vellent	nollent	irent

Perfect (whether -ed)

fúerim	potúerim	volúerim	nolúerim	ierim
fúeris	potúeris	volúeris	volúeris	ieris
fúerit	potúerit	volúerit	nolúerit	ierit
fuérimus	potuérimus	voluérimus	noluérimus	iérimus
fuéritis	potuéritis	voluéritis	noluéritis	iéritis
fúerint	potúerint	volúerint	nolúerint	ierint

Pluperfect (whether had -ed)

fuíssem	potuíssem	voluíssem	noluíssem	issem
fuísses	potuísses	voluísses	noluísses	isses
fuísset	potuísset	voluísset	noluísset	isset
fuissémus	potuissémus	voluissémus	noluissémus	issemus
fuissétis	potuissétis	voluissétis	noluissétis	issetis
fuíssent	potuíssent	voluíssent	noluíssent	issent

Roman Numerals	Cardinals	Ordinals
I	únus, a, um	prímus, a, um
II	duo, duae, duo	secundus, a, um
III	trés, tria	tertius, a, um
IV	quattor	quártus, a, um
V	quínque	quíntus, a, um
VI	sex	sextus, a, um
VII	septem	septimus, a, um
VIII	octó	octávus, a, um
IX	novem	nónus, a, um
X	decem	decimus, a, um
XI	úndecem	úndecimus, a, um
XII	duodecem	duodecimus, a, um
XIII	tredecem	tertius, a um decimus, a, um
XIV	quattuordecem	quártus, a, um decimus, a, um
XV	quíndecem	quíntus, a, um decimus, a, um
XVI	sédecem	sextus, a, um decimus, a, um
XVII	septendecem	septimus, a, um decimus, a, um
XVIII	duodévígintí	duodévícésimus, a, um
XIX	úndévígintí	úndévícésimus, a, um
XX	vígintí	vícésimus, a, um
XXI	vígintí unus	vícésimus, a, um primus, a, um
XXX	trígintá	trícésimus, a, um
XL	quadrágintá	quadrágésimus, a, um
L	quinquágintá	quínquágésimus, a, um
LX	sexágintá	sexágésimus, a, um
LXX	septuágintá	septuágésimus, a, um
LXXX	octógintá	octógésimus, a, um
XC	nónágintá	nónágésimus, a, um
C	centum	centésimus, a, um
CC	ducentí	ducentésimus, a, um
CCC	trecentí	trecentésimus, a, um
CD	quadringentí	quadringentésimus, a, um
D	quíngentí	quíngentésimus, a, um
DC	sescentí	sescentésimus, a, um
DCC	septingentí	septingentésimus, a, um
DCCC	octingentí	octingentésimus, a, um
CM	nóngentí	nóngentésimus, a, um
M	mílle	míllésimus, a, um
MM	duo milliá	bis míllésimus, a, um

Latin Exercises

Why study Latin since it is not spoken anywhere today? Since Latin is the root of many languages, you will recognize many words commonly used in English, Spanish, French and Italian. Internet, facsimile [fax], computer, audio, video, analysis, digital, incognito and et cetera are Latin words.

This book will greatly assist those who attend the Latin Mass, pray the Divine Office (*Breviarium Romanum)* or are studying for the priesthood. It will make you proficient in English and dramatically improve your vocabulary and diction. Latin will save you time since you won't have to use a dictionary as often since most English words have Latin roots.

Latin nouns and verbs are like Roman legions, each have a special place and role. The language is precise and consistent and actually quite simple.

Your success at understanding and being proficient in Latin will depend on memorization. This includes nouns: their translation, gender (to properly match adjectives) and declension endings, and verbs: their conjugation, endings and four principal parts. This book will concentrate on commonly used verbs and nouns. Additional words are found in the word lists for your use as needed.

As you study and memorize, you will enjoy the language and will save hours of time by not having to look up words or endings. Daily spend about 10 minutes on exercises and 10 minutes on memorizing. Exercises can be done in order, by odd or even numbers or mixed. Once you or your class grasps what was covered, move on. Some answers are given to assist you.

To facilitate learning Latin, you may write in this book and then use it for future reference. If your instructor chooses, exercises can be copied and handed out, making the book available for students for the following year.

By the time you finish, you will have a working use of the language and be able to translate, write and speak in Latin. Have fun! Habe jocus!

Sentences are Made of Parts

Nouns: (persons, places or things) student, teacher, home, school, book, table

     discipulus, magister, domus, schola, liber, mensa

Adjectives: (words that describe nouns), good, bad, new, old, large, small

     bonus, malus, novus, antiquus, magnus, parvulus

Conjunctions: (unite nouns) and, either... or, neither... nor, both, therefore

     et, aut... aut, nec... nec, ambo, ideo

Prepositions: to, for, by, with, without, before, after, under, over, across

     ad, pro, a (ab), cum, sine, ante, post, sub, supra, trans

Adverbs: (often have –ly) carefully, slowly, quickly, secretly, openly

     caute, tarde, cito, clam, aperte

Verbs: (action words) go, come, walk, sit, work, pray

     ite, veni, ambula, sede, labora, ora

Adjectives describe **nouns**, **conjunctions** link phrases and sentences are formed by using **verbs**, **adverbs** and **prepositions**. You will learn about one group at a time so you can see how sentences are created.

pagina III   # Declensions

1) How many declensions does Latin have? **five**

2) Which declensions are feminine? _____ _____

3) Which declensions are masculine? _____ _____

4) Which declension is both masculine and feminine? _____

5) What are the neuter declensions? _____ _____ _____

6) What are the three genders in Latin? _____ _____ _____

7) Why do nouns have gender? _____

8) Is gender in Latin always accurate? _____

9) Declensions list endings in singular and _____.

pagina IV   **Cases**

1) The vocative case is used in Latin for **direct address**.

2) The subject of the sentence is always in the _____ case.

3) The accusative case is used for the _____ _____.

4) Accusative case is used with prepositions that take the _____ case.

5) The _____ case is used as the object of prepositions that takes the

_____ case.

6) The dative case is used for the _____ _____. In English, the

words ____ and ____ are often used.

7) _____ case shows possession, in English using the word ____ or 's.

8) Give the vocative for: a. amica b. medicus c. pater d. spiritus

    See pagina (page) IV (4) and check declension lists pp. V-IX.

9) Decline nouns listed below in all cases singular and plural or choose words

    from each declension (including neuter) from lists on paginae XIII-XXX.

a. regina, ae	1st declension (feminine)
b. discipulus, í	2nd declension (masculine)
c. festum, í	2nd declension neuter
d. canis, canis (m/f)	3rd declension
e. lumen, luminis	3rd declension neuter
f. impetus, ú	4th declension (masculine)
g. gelú, ús	4th declension neuter
h. fidés, eí	5th declension

pagina V

First Declension

	Singular	Plural
nominative	regina	reginae
accusative		
ablative		
dative		
genitive		

pagina VI

Second Declension

	Singular	Plural
nominative	medicus	medicí
accusative		
ablative		
dative		
genitive		

pagina VII

Second Declension Neuter

	Singular	Plural
nominative	aedificium	aedificia
accusative		
ablative		
dative		
genitive		

pagina VIII

Third Declension

	Singular	Plural
nominative	canis	canes
accusative		
ablative		
dative		
genitive		

pagina VIII

Third Declension Neuter

	Singular	Plural
nominative	**flumen**	**flumines**
accusative		
ablative		
dative		
genitive		

pagina IX

Fourth Declension

	Singular	Plural
nominative	**intellectus**	**intellectús**
accusative		
ablative		
dative		
genitive		

pagina IX

Fourth Declension Neuter

	Singular	Plural
nominative	**gelú**	**gelua**
accusative		
ablative		
dative		
genitive		

pagina IX

Fifth Declension

	Singular	Plural
nominative	**glaciés**	**glaciés**
accusative		
ablative		
dative		
genitive		

paginae XIII-XXX   **Understanding Cases**

list to use	declension	case(s)	sing. or pl.	translate
1) manú (anatomy)	fourth	ablative	singular	with the hand
2) cimex (animals)				
3) puellae (people) (three possible)				
a)				
b)				
c)				
4) villárum (building)				
5) timore (characteristics)				
6) farinam (food)				
7) lignís (building) (two possible)				
a)				
b)				
8) galeas (military)				
9) genús (three possible)				
a)				
b)				
c)				
10) mulieribus (two possible)				
a)				
b)				
11) rosís (two possible)				
a)				
b)				
12) sancte				
13) specieí				
14) sede				
15) pacem				
16) adjutorium				

pagina X   # Placement

1) The **subject** is usually the first word in the sentence.

2) The _____ is usually the last word in the sentence.

3) The _____ _____ usually follows the subject.

3) The _____ _____ usually follows the indirect object.

4) The _____ of _____ follows the direct object.

5) _____ and _____ are used whenever needed.

pagina XI **Preposition**	**Case** **accusative** or **ablative**?	**Translate**
cum	ablative	with
sine		
ad		
ante		
in		
post		
ab		
circum		
contra		
in		
per		
supra		
pro		
trans		
inter		
intra		
sub		
secundum		
propter		
ultra		

e (is used before): **consonants**

ex (is used before):_____

ab (is used before):_____

a (is used before):_____

in (is used with the ablative means):_____

in (is used with the accusative means):_____

Translate

1) ad montes (world list)
   to the mountains

2) per silvas (world list)

3) canis caldus cum sinapis (food list)

4) in Paradisum (religious words list)
   both are accusative

5) ex cathedrá (things list)

6) ad Jesum per Mariam (this is easy)

7) cum amicis (people list)

8) sine fine (military words)

9) ad altare Deí (religious words list)

10) coram Deum (religious words)

Using nouns in the vocabulary lists on pp. XIII-XXX, give 10 examples of a preposition followed by a noun in either the accusative or ablative case.

Then translate. for example: per montibus through the mountains

	Latin	English	case
1) ante	**ante scholam**	**before school**	**acc.**
2) trans			
3) super			
4) sub			
5) sine			
6) cum			
7) ab			
8) ex			
9) cum			
10) inter			

Translate sections of the Gospel for the Annunciation Luke 1: 26-39

1) **a** Deó (religious words list)   **from God**

2) **in** civitatem (world list) Galilaeae (of Galilee)

3) **ad** virginem (people list)

4) **de** domó (building list)

5) **ad eam** (personal pronoun—pagina xxxi)

6) benedicta (adj) **tu** (pers. pro. p. xxxi) **in** (**among**) mulieribus (people list).

7) gratiam **apud** Deum

8) **in** domó Jacob (of Jacob)

9) **ad** angelum

10) **in te** (personal pronoun—pagina xxxi)

pagina XII   **Give the Nominative Singular Ending for**:

1) 3rd declension   **it varies**   5) 3rd declension neuter

2) 1st declension   6) 5th declension

3) 2nd declension   7) 2nd declension neuter

4) 4th declension   8) 4th declension neuter

pagina XII   **Give the Genitive Singular Ending for:**

1-2) 4th declension and 4th declension neuter   **ús ús**

3-4) 2nd declension and 2nd declension neuter

5-6) 3rd declension and 3rd declension neuter

7) 5th declension

8) 1st declension

pagina XIII   **Give Declension and Translate** (anatomy list)

1) genu, ús   **4th   knee**   9) auris, auris

2) mens, mentis   10) brachium, ií

3) oculus, í   11) lingua, ae

4) calvaria, ae   12) ós, oris

5) digitus, í

6) manús, ús

7) venter, ventris

8) faciés, eí

13) capillus, í

14) scapulae, árum

15) dens, dentis

16) os, ossis

pagina XIV **Give Genitive and Translate** (animal list)

1) cancer, **cancerí of the crab**

2) feles,

3) canis,

4) musca,

5) cetus,

6) lupus,

7) cimex,

8) apis,

9) avis,

10) porcus,

pagina XV **Give Genitive and Translate** (building list)

1) aedificium, **aedificií of the building**

2) ecclesia,

3) casa,

4) horreum,

5) fenestra,

6) taberna,

7) janua,

8) villa,

9) fons,

10) porta,

pagina XVI **Give Genitive and Translate** (proprietates)

1) monitio, **monitionis warning**

2) amicitia,

3) décor,

4) odium,

5) fiducia,

pagina XVII **Translate** (vestes)

1) calceamentum **shoe, sandal**

2) instita

3) subucula

4) bracae

5) pilleus

Read the section on adjectives: pp. 37-39. Adjectives are very similar to nouns, but only have three declensions, plus 2nd and 3rd neuter forms.

Adjectives are listed on pages 37, 40-43. They agree with nouns they modify in gender, number and case and usually follow nouns.

Write in Latin (Scribe in Latine)

(Use materials, religious and adjective lists.)

translate   give gender, number and case

1) strong metal   **mettalum durum   neuter   singular   nominative**

2) heavy iron

3) hot lead

4) soft gold

5) shiny silver

6) hard wood

7) building materials

8) new brass

9) beautiful pearl

10) long rope

(religious words list) (adjectives list)

11) St. Cletus (2nd declension)

12) St. Barbara (1st declension)

13) Holy God (religious adjectives precede nouns)

14) small chapel

15) large church

16) holy oil

17) my youth [make accusative] (people list)

18) Holy Mary

19) Blessed Trinity

20) my fault

Translate into English (Verte in Anglice)

1) Sancte Joseph

2) Corona (et cetera list) gloriae (genitive case).

3) Mulier amicta (adj.) sole (world list) et luna (world list) sub pedibus
   (anatomy) ejus (pers. pronoun) et capite (anatomy) ejus coronam
   (things list) stellárum (world list) duodecim (measurement list).

Translate (cibus et adjective lists)

Some of these words are nouns so they don't agree in gender number or case.

1) ariena flava   **yellow banana**

2) bacca caerulea

3) carnis cruda

4) nitrum uva

5) panis angelicus

6) esca bona

7) crustum bacca nigra

8) malum condimentum dulcis

9) collyrida chocolatum

10) angelus esca collyrida

11) lardum et (and) ovi

12) frumentum et lac

Scribe in Latine (animalia, verba religiosae and adjective lists)

1) red bull   **taurus rubrus**

2) black cat

3) great white shark

4) blue whale

5) red fox

6) Lamb of God

7) sheep and goats

8) brown cattle

9) black widow spider

10) green frogs

11) sacred orders

12) great saints

13) pious women

14) high altar

15) wise men

16) holy joy

17) deep humility

18) highest virtue

19) peace of soul

20) Blessed Trinity

paginae XX-XXI

Numerous military terms are found in the psalms of David for those who pray the Divine Office. Others will occasionaly see these terms so you should become familiar with them. Find the Latin counterpart for the English words in the list below, then give the nominative singular and plural forms.

1) arrow   **sagitta**   **sagittae**

2) shield

3) battleline

4) sword

5) battle

paginae XXI-XXII **Find the Latin word for**:

1) father	**pater**	9) woman (1)
2) mother (1)		10) young man
3) mother (1)		11) young lady
4) brother		12) boy
5) sister		13) girl
6) man (1)		14) grandmother
7) man (1)		15) student
8) woman (1)		

paginae XXII-XXIV **Give the English word for**:

1) Deus	**God**	7) vidua
2) angelus		8) virgo
3) divus		9) senex
4) papa		10) rex
5) episcopus		11) regina
6) parocheus		12) judex

Common Ecclesiastical Latin Words

Pater noster: Our Father
pater, patris m: father (noun) noster, nostra, nostrum: our (adjective)
They agree in gender (masculine) number (singular) and case (nominative)

Ave Maria: Hail Mary
ave: hail (interjection) Maria, ae f: Mary (noun)

Bone Pastor: Good Shepherd
bonus, a, um: good (adj) vocative (e replaces us) pastor, is m: pastor (noun)

per Dominum nostrum Jesum Christum
per takes accusative Dominus, í m: lord (noun) noster, nostra, nostrum: our
Jesus, us m: Jesus Christus, í m: Christ

Regina Caeli: Queen of Heaven
regina, ae f: queen (nominative) caelum, í n: Heaven (genitive)

pagina XLVI   # Using Conjunctions

	word list	translation
1) felesque canes	animalia	**cats and dogs**
2) bonus aut malus	adjectives	
3) ager et fluetum	orbis	
4) aves atque apes	animalia	
5) corpus ac anima	anatomia verba religiosae	
6) crustulí et crema	cibus	
7) aut vita aut mors	res	
8) aut bubula aut pullus	cibus	
9) et ostia et fenestra	aedificium	
10) leones et tigres ac ursae	animalia	
11) nec pluvia nec nix	caelum	
12) Filoque		

Scribe in Latine

1) Heaven and earth. **caelum et terra** or **caelum terraque**

2) Either today or tomorrow. (Use adverbs for today and tomorrow found on paginae XLIX et L.)

3) For this is My Body. (Use the conjunction **enim** and the neuter, singular, nom. form of the demonstrative pronoun **hic, haec, hoc** on pagina XXXII.)

4) Tantum ergo. (Use adjective **tantus, a, um.**)

VOCABULARY REVIEW

See how well you studied by giving the English word for:

Extra credit: give declension and gender. Remember both are important.

1) caput, capitis (think of captain)

2) mens, mentis (think of mental)

3) corpus, corporis (think of corporal)

4) lingua, linguae

5) oculus, oculí (think of ocular)

6) agnus, agní

7) equus, equí (think of equestrian)

8) canis, canis (think of canine)

9) feles, felis (think of feline)

10) aedificium, aedificií (think of edifice)

11) casa, ae (like Spanish)

12) ecclesia, ae (think of ecclesiastical)

13) fons, fontis

14) janua, januae

15) dolor, doloris

16) timor, timoris

17) esca, escae

18) frumentum, frumentí

19) mel, mellis

20) cena, cenae

21) argentum, argentí

22) aurum, aurí

23) clamor, clamoris

24) gladius, gladií

25) impetus, impetús

26) periculum, periculí

27) proelium, proelií

28) cithara, citharae

29) tuba, tubae

30) adolescenta, adolescentae

31) adolescentus, adolescentí

32) agricola, agricolae

33) amicus, amicí (amigo in Spanish)

Learning How to Use the Verb "sum"

The words: "is," "are," "was" and "were" are commonly used in English. In order to easily learn Latin verbs, simple sentences will be used.

Present tense is used to describe actions going on now. "I see." "You play." "He or she walks." "It is new." "We sing." "You are good." "They are fast."

Latin differs from English in that the verb is usually the last word in the sentence. Also, verbs have four principal parts that are used to make up other tenses. The principal part used: I, II, III or IV, and the endings added to a verb determine its meaning.

In Latin the verb "to be" (is, are, was, were) is irregular—it is formed (conjugated) differently than other verbs. Even so, it is a great place to start.

Romans were very methodical.

Verbs are set up in groups of six using the personal pronouns:

1st person singular	I	1st person plural	we
2nd person singular	you	2nd person plural	you
3rd person singular	he, she, it	3rd person plural	they

Indicative Mood (used for common speech)
Present Tense
Active Voice

Latin	English	Latin	English
sum	I am	**sumus**	we are
es	you are	**estis**	you are
est	he, she, it is	**sunt**	they are

Writing Your First Latin Sentences

Below are examples of 1st, 2nd and 3rd person. The word "is" means equals. Therefore, the subject and the word modifying it with a form of "be" use the *same* gender, number and case as the subject: the nominative case.

Use personal pronouns on pagina XXXI & adjectives on paginae XL-XLIII.

1) I am happy.

   Ego (nom. 1st person sing.) **felix** (nominative) **sum** (1st person sing.).

2) You are brave.

3) He is strong.

4) She is kind.

5) It is hidden.

6) We are cold. pronoun, adjective, present tense form of be (sum)

For males use nominative, masculine plural form. **Nos frigidí sumus.**

or because the pronoun is contained in the verb: **Frigidí sumus.**

For females-nom. fem. pl. form: **Nos frigidae sumus.** or **Frigidae sumus.**

7) You are right.

8) They are serious.

9) The farmer (nom. case) and (conjunction) the stranger (nom. case) are (form of "sum" 3rd person plural) in (preposition) the field (ablative).

10) The car (or chariot) is in the garage (barn).

11) My (meus, a, um) aunt and grandmother are in the store.

12) Your uncle is on a boat at the lake.

13) My parents are good.

14) Angels are in Heaven.

15) Life is short (brevis, is, e); eternity is long. (longus, a, um)

16) Banana is a fruit.

17) Snow is cold. (Use the same gender, number and case for the adjective.)

18) Soldiers are in the camp.

Review Translate into English (Verte in Anglice)

1) Domine non sum dignus (adjective).

2) Corona (res list) vitae. (et cetera list)

3) Opera (opus, operis see et cetera list) vestra (adj.) bona. (adj.)

4) Coram (preposition) hominibus. (homo, hominis-people list)

5) Coram Angelis Dei. (religious list).

6) Urbs et orbis. (world list)

7) Cervi (animals list) in silvá (world list) sunt.

8) Lacus (world list) profundus (adjective list) est.

References

http://www2.fiu.edu/~mirandas/bios-b.htm#Bacci Downloaded on 3/22/12 at 4:08 PM. (Cardinal Bacci invented the Latin word for chewing gum.)

Beard, Henry. *Latin for All Occasions.* New York: Villard Books, 1991.

Breviarium Romanum Pars Aestiva, H. Dessain: Mechliniae, 1955.

Diamond, Wilfrid. *Liturgical Latin.* New York: Benziger Brothers, 1941.

Fairbairn, Donald. *Understanding Language: A Guide for Beginning Students in Greek and Latin,* Washington DC: Catholic University of America Press, 2011.

www.georgetown.edu/irvinemj/classics203/resources/latin.lex

Griffith, Rev. Paul. *Priest's New Ritual,* New York: Kenedy, 1947.

Henle, *Latin Grammar,* Chicago: Loyola University Press, 1958.

Kidd, MA D. *Collins Latin Gem Dictionary: Latin-English: English-Latin,* London: Collins: 1957.

Konus, Rev. William. *Dictionary of the New Psalter of Pope Pius XII,* Newman Press: Westminster, 1959.

Kuhnmuench, SJ Otto. *Liturgical Latin,* Chicago: Loyola University Press, 1939.

http://www.latin-dictionary.net/search/latin/

Latin Vocabulary Cards, Dayton, Ohio: Vis-Ed Association.

Marchant, MA J. and Joseph Charles, BA. *Cassel's Latin Dictionary,* Oxford: Cassel and Company, LTD.

Missale Romanum, Marietti: Turonis, 1957.

North, Eric. *Book of a Thousand Tongues,* London: United Bible Societies, 1939.

Scanlan, Cora AM and Charles Scanlan. *Latin Grammar,* Rockford: Tan, 1976.

Scanlan, Cora AM and Charles Scanlan. *Second Latin,* Rockford: Tan, 1976.

Stelten, Leo, *Dictionary of Ecclesiastical Latin,* Peabody, MA: Hendrickson Publishers, 1997.

Stone, Jon. *Latin for the Illiterati: Exorcising the Ghosts of a Dead Language,* Routledge: New York, 1996.

Traupman, PhD John. *New College Latin and English Dictionary,* New York: Bantam Books Inc., 1966.

Wheelock, Fredric. Richard LaFleur revision editor, *Wheelock's Latin,* New York: HarperCollins Publishers, Inc. 1995.